CHINESE COOKING

Gail Weinshel Katz

WEATHERVANE
BOOKS

I would like to thank my friends and relatives who contributed some of their favorite recipes to this book. I also thank Anni Schneider for her assistance and, most of all, my husband and children for their eager willingness to sample these recipes as I tested them.

contents

introduction

Szechwan, Canton, Peking, Fukien! What really is Chinese cooking? The above are four different areas in China, each known for its own special type of cooking. Chinese cooking is as varied as American cooking. There is one thing, however, that separates Chinese cuisine from all others and that is its dependence on vegetables cooked quickly to maintain crispness. To that, add careful preparation before cooking, contrasting tastes and textures, and esthetically pleasing presentation at the table. There you have Chinese cooking.

The geographic climatological factors that affect the availability of raw supplies also dictate the kinds of foods for which each area or region of China are known.

The Szechwan, or inland region, is the area for Szechwan pepper, called *fagara*. It seems to make its presence known as it "sneaks up" on one. At first there isn't much taste and then . . .!! Some of the best-known dishes from this region are Szechwan Beef, Chicken with Walnuts, and Szechwan Pork.

The Canton, or southern region, is the area from which the first Chinese emigrated in large numbers in the mid-nineteenth century. Thus, Cantonese cooking became popular in Chinese restaurants in Europe, Southeast Asia, and America. This is subtly seasoned and is the least greasy of all Chinese cooking. The Cantonese are excellent at stir-frying. Nuts and mushrooms and highly concentrated chicken broth are used in this region. Sharks' Fin Soup is a Cantonese specialty. Some of the best-known specialties from here are Egg Rolls and Egg Foo Yong.

The northern, or Peking region, is well-known for deep-fried and sautéed foods. Delicately seasoned foods, sweet-and-sour dishes, and noodle dishes are some of their specialties. Of course, many of us are familiar with Peking Duck, for which this area is famous.

The Fukien, or coastal region, is well-known for excellent fish dishes and soups. This area uses lots of vegetables and gently spiced concoctions of meat, fowl, and seafood.

Most of the recipes in this book are not complicated, and, even if you have never done any Chinese cooking, you should find them trouble-free.

Tips to remember in Chinese cooking

The foods you are cooking should be as fresh as possible. If you have a choice of buying a canned or fresh vegetable, buy the fresh. The results are worth it!

Prepare all the ingredients before cooking is begun. You will need a little patience, but you'll find this is a must. Once cooking has begun, you won't have time to cut vegetables.

When you begin the cooking, it must be watched—don't overcook! Remember, Chinese cooking is rapid cooking at a high temperature. Chinese frown on soggy meat or vegetables.

Use vegetable oil in all recipes unless otherwise specified. It can withstand high temperatures without smoking or burning.

Partially frozen meat is easier to cut into neat, thin slices.

The ingredients in each dish should be of uniform size.

Each dish should have a pleasant aroma, and at each meal the dishes should be varied for texture and taste. For instance, serve a crispy dish and a smooth dish, and a spicy dish with a bland dish, etc. Of course, these should all be colorful and pleasing to the eye.

Cornstarch is the thickener most often used in Chinese cuisine, because cornstarch thickens well without making the sauce pasty. Thin sauce cannot be picked up with chopsticks, but if the sauce is thickened with cornstarch, it will then adhere to the food and can be enjoyed when eating with chopsticks.

A typical informal Chinese meal has 4 courses. A formal meal might have as many as 10 or 12 courses. Here is a guide to figure how many people can be served from a particular dish. If the vegetables and meat (or fish) in any one dish total one pound, three or four people can be served from that dish. For two pounds of vegetables and meat or fish, figure on serving 6 to 8 people. For three pounds, 9 to 12 people can be served. This is, of course, when serving a variety of dishes.

If you're going to be cooking Chinese, your best investment would be in the purchase of a wok. Its conical shape, with the heat centered at the bottom, makes it ideal for so many things—deep-frying, stir-frying (quick cooking of small pieces of meat and vegetables), sautéeing, and simmering; with the addition of a cake rack you have an ideal utensil for steaming. The wok will withstand very high heat, uses less oil than a regular frying pan, and is ideal for small or large batches of food.

You may also want to purchase a few utensils to aid in the preparation of the meals. Wooden spoons are ideal for using two at a time when stir-frying. Brass strainers are ideal for spooning deep-fried foods out of the cooking utensil. Spatulas are needed for turning foods, and a chinese cleaver is handy for slicing, mincing, shredding, cubing, or chopping food to any size.

By all means be creative with Chinese cooking. Try your own combinations of ingredients. Most of all, have fun! The entire family, for instance, may enjoy cooking in the wok! With a little patience and some imagination you can master this delicious and beautiful art.

guide to unusual ingredients

Bamboo shoots: Shoots of the tropical bamboo. Can be purchased canned in supermarkets. Refrigerate in water in covered jar. They will keep approximately 2 weeks if water is changed daily.

Bean sprouts: Sprouts of the mung bean. You can purchase them canned at supermarkets, or, preferably, fresh from the produce department. You can also grow your own. See recipe in this book.

Bok choy: A variety of Chinese cabbage. It has smooth white stalks and dark-green leaves. Can be purchased in some supermarkets or in Oriental food stores.

Celeriac root: A variety of celery. It can be purchased in some supermarkets or in specialty stores.

Chinese cabbage (or celery cabbage): One of the oldest food crops of China. It has wide, thick leaves that form a long, cylindrical head. It can be purchased in some supermarkets and in Oriental food stores.

Dried black mushrooms (Chinese mushrooms): Available in cellophane bags in some supermarkets and in Oriental food stores. Soak them in warm water for 20 to 30 minutes, remove stems, and slice.

Dried sharks' fins: Long, translucent threads of dried cartilage from the fins of sharks. May be purchased in Chinese food stores.

Duck sauce (or plum sauce): Sauce with sweet-and-pungent flavor made from apricots, plums, chili, sugar, and vinegar. It's available in bottles in supermarkets.

Gingerroot: Knobby brown root. It is sold by weight in some supermarkets in the produce section and in Oriental food stores. It will keep in the refrigerator for several weeks if wrapped well.

Hoisin sauce: A thick, sweet, brownish-red sauce made from soybeans, flour, sugar, and spices. It is sold in cans in some supermarkets and in Oriental food stores. Refrigerate in covered jar after opening. It will keep for several months.

MSG (monosodium glutamate): A white crystalline powder. It is used to flavor foods.

Oyster sauce: A thick brown sauce made from oysters, salt, and soybeans. It can be purchased in bottles in some supermarkets and in Oriental food stores. Refrigerate after opening.

Rice wine: Made from fermented rice. It is available at large liquor stores or Oriental food stores. You can substitute sherry.

Safflower oil: Available in bottles in supermarkets.

Savoy cabbage: Small, light-green cabbage. Its leaves are heavily veined. You can substitute regular cabbage. It is available in some supermarkets and some Oriental food stores.

Sesame-seed oil: Made from roasted sesame seeds. It is sold in bottles. It's available at supermarkets or Oriental food stores. The sesame-seed oil purchased at a supermarket may be milder than that available in Oriental food stores.

Snow peas: Flat green pea pods with very small peas inside. The entire pod is edible. Remove strings before cooking. Available in many supermarkets and in Oriental food stores.

Soy sauce: Pungent brown liquid made from fermented soybeans, wheat, yeast, and salt. It can be purchased in bottles in supermarkets. Please use a good-quality soy sauce in your Chinese cooking.

Star anise: Dry, brown, licorice-flavored spice. Available at Oriental food stores.

Sugared ginger (or candied ginger): Sold in cellophane bags or boxes at some supermarkets and in Oriental food stores or gourmet food stores.

Transparent noodles: Also called silver threads, cellophane noodles, and translucent noodles. Available in supermarkets or Oriental food stores.

Water chestnuts: White crunchy bulbs, about the size of a walnut. Available canned at supermarkets. Refrigerate in water in covered jar after opening. Change the water daily. They will keep 3 to 4 weeks. You may be able to purchase them fresh at Chinese specialty stores. They will keep refrigerated for several days.

White rice vinegar: Sweeter and milder than American vinegar. Available in Oriental food stores.

Won Ton: A dough made from flour, water, and eggs. It is formed into squares. They are filled and deep-fried or cooked in boiling water and used in soup. They can be purchased at some supermarkets and Oriental food stores, or you can make your own.

appetizers

won ton

½ pound pork, minced
¼ cup fresh mushrooms, minced
1 tablespoon scallion, minced
¼ teaspoon salt
⅛ teaspoon freshly ground black pepper
1 egg yolk
Won ton squares
Peanut oil

Mix minced pork, mushrooms, and scallion with salt, pepper, and egg yolk. Place ½ teaspoonful of the mixture in center of won ton square. Fold one corner up over the filling at an angle to make two askew triangles. Pull the bottom corners of the triangles gently down below their base. Overlap the tips of the two corners slightly and pinch them together. Fry in hot peanut oil and drain. Serve with Chinese mustard or catsup mixed with a little horseradish.

Makes approximately 120 won ton.

chinese stuffed mushrooms

24 large mushrooms, stems removed
1 pound ground meat
4 tablespoons chopped scallions
3½ tablespoons soy sauce, divided
⅛ teaspoon salt
Freshly ground black pepper to taste
1½ tablespoons flour
1¼ cups beef broth

Wash mushrooms, remove stems, and put mushrooms aside. Chop together the meat and scallions, until fine. Add 1 tablespoon soy sauce, salt, pepper, and flour. Shape mixture into small balls and stuff mushrooms. Heat large skillet to medium heat. Add remaining soy sauce and beef broth. Place mushrooms in skillet stuffed-side-up, cover and let cook for about 20 minutes, or until meat is done.
Makes 24 stuffed mushrooms.

appetizers wrapped in bacon

8 slices bacon, cut in half
1 pound chicken livers, cut in half
1 6-ounce can whole water chestnuts, drained and sliced

Lay bacon slices flat and place chicken livers and water chestnuts on tops and roll up. Secure with toothpicks. Place appetizers in small amount of hot oil in frying pan or wok and cook until bacon is browned.
Makes 4 servings.

cocktail meatballs

1 20-ounce can pineapple chunks
1 jar red cherry jelly or preserves
¼ cup catsup
3 whole cloves
1 stick cinnamon
1 teaspoon salt
1 teaspoon cornstarch
1 tablespoon soy sauce
1 pound ground chuck made into cooked meatballs

Drain pineapple and reserve juice. Combine juice with jelly or preserves, catsup, cloves, cinnamon and salt. Heat to boiling. Dissolve cornstarch in enough liquid (either water or a small amount of the pineapple-juice mixture) to make a smooth paste and stir into the boiling mixture. Cook until cornstarch thickens and clears.
Add the pineapple chunks and soy sauce. Pour over the cooked meatballs in a chafing dish and serve warm.
Makes approximately 4 servings as an appetizer.

sandie's chicken wings

These are delicious!

1 10-ounce bottle soy sauce
2 teaspoons freshly grated ginger, or 1 teaspoon powdered ginger
2 cloves garlic, minced
⅓ cup brown sugar
1 teaspoon dark mustard
24 chicken wings
Garlic powder

Mix together soy sauce, ginger, garlic, brown sugar, and mustard. Blend well. Marinate chicken wings in mixture for two hours or longer. Drain wings, reserving marinade. Bake 1½ hours at 350°F, turning and basting with marinade frequently. Sprinkle with garlic powder and place under broiler to get crispy for a minute or two just before serving.

Makes 8 to 12 servings as appetizer or 4 to 5 servings as main dish.

jean's oriental chicken livers

These chicken livers are delicious!

8 ounces chicken livers, cut in half
⅓ cup soy sauce
½ cup flour
1 small onion, sliced, or onion flakes

Marinate chicken livers overnight in soy sauce. Remove livers from marinade and dredge in flour. Heat small amount of oil in frying pan and fry livers and onion until browned. Serve as an appetizer, or with rice as a main course.

Makes approximately 4 servings as an appetizer or 2 servings as a main course.

scallops chinese-style

1 cup soy sauce
1 tablespoon lemon juice
2 teaspoons fresh gingerroot, finely chopped, or substitute powdered ginger
2 tablespoons sugar
¼ teaspoon MSG
1 pound scallops, cut into bite-size pieces

In large saucepan combine soy sauce, lemon juice, ginger, sugar, and MSG. Bring to a boil. Add scallops and cook over medium-high heat until all the liquid has evaporated.

Makes approximately 25 appetizers.

chinese sweet-and-sour sauce

Serve this with chicken, beef, pork, or seafood.

4 tablespoons catsup
¼ cup brown sugar
2 tablespoons soy sauce
3 tablespoons wine vinegar
2 tablespoons dry white wine
2 tablespoons cornstarch dissolved in ½ cup cold water

Combine catsup, sugar, soy sauce, vinegar and wine in saucepan. Bring to a boil. Add the cornstarch dissolved in water to the sauce. Cook over low heat, stirring constantly, until sauce has thickened. Makes about 1¼ cups sauce.

sweet-and-sour plum sauce

½ cup water
1 cup plum jelly
2 tablespoons catsup
2 tablespoons vinegar

Place ingredients in saucepan and stir. Bring to boil. Serve warm. Makes approximately 1½ cups sauce.

egg-roll skins

18 eggs
3 tablespoons cornstarch
3 teaspoons salt
2¼ cups water
Oil

Beat eggs. Add cornstarch and salt. Beat in water. Heat oil in bottom of 8-inch frying pan or wok and pour about ¼ cup of batter into pan. Fry lightly, turn and fry on other side. Makes approximately 24 skins.

sandie's vegetarian egg rolls

Experiment with this recipe. These are very good!

Vegetables such as:
  cabbage   **fresh mushrooms**
  bok choy   **onions**
  celery   **scallions**
  carrots   **green pepper**
                                 bean sprouts

Use as many of the above vegetables as you wish, in whatever amounts you desire. Shred or finely chop all the vegetables. Stir-fry quickly in small amount of oil. Add soy sauce to taste, garlic powder and some peanut butter. Fill egg roll skins, or won ton skins (for cocktail size) and fry in oil in wok (or deep frypan). Serve immediately or freeze and warm in oven before serving.

sauce
Apricot preserves
Plum preserves   **Dijon mustard**
Soy sauce   **Peanut butter**

Combine amounts of above ingredients to taste. Some prefer the sauce somewhat sweet, while others like it sharp.

Tilt skillet to spread egg-roll batter evenly.

Divide filling among egg-roll squares.

Fold 2 opposite corners of egg rolls toward middle.

Fry egg rolls in hot oil in deep pan until done.

egg rolls

for dough
½ **pound flour**
1½ **cups water**
Salt
1½ **teaspoons peanut oil**

for filling
½ **pound green cabbage**
1 **leek**
1 **medium onion**
1 **8-ounce can bamboo shoots**
1 **4-ounce can mushrooms**

4 **tablespoons oil**
4 **ounces ground beef**
4 **ounces ground pork**
2 **cups fresh bean sprouts**
4 **tablespoons soy sauce**
2 **tablespoons sherry**
Salt
Cayenne pepper

Peanut oil
Beaten egg yolks
6 **cups oil for deep frying**

Place flour in a bowl. Slowly stir in water, making sure that you always stir in the same direction. Add salt and 1½ teaspoons peanut oil and cover bowl. Let rest for 30 minutes. Meanwhile prepare filling. Wash and drain cabbage and leek and cut into thin slices. Chop onion. Drain bamboo shoots and cut into fine strips. Drain and coarsely chop mushrooms. In skillet heat 4 tablespoons oil and add ground meats; cook until lightly browned. Stir in cabbage, leek, onion and bamboo shoots. Cook for 5 minutes. Add mushrooms and bean sprouts and cook for an additional 2 minutes. Season to taste with soy sauce, sherry, salt and cayenne pepper. Remove from heat and set aside.

Brush an 8-inch skillet with peanut oil. Pour in ⅛ of the egg roll dough; tilt skillet to spread batter evenly. Over low heat cook until set. Turn out onto moistened paper toweling. Cover with another moistened paper towel. Continue until all dough is used up. Cut egg roll rounds into 6-inch squares. Divide filling among the eight egg rolls. Fold two opposite corners of egg rolls towards middle. Starting with corner closest to you, roll up egg roll. Brush inside of opposite corner with small amount of beaten egg yolk; seal egg roll. Heat oil in deep frypan. Add rolls and fry until done. Put paper toweling on cake rack, place egg rolls on rack and drain. Keep them warm and serve on preheated platter.

Makes 8 egg rolls.

egg rolls

You can purchase ready-made egg roll skins in supermarkets or Oriental specialty stores.

dipping batter
1 egg
1 tablespoon cornstarch
1½ teaspoons baking powder
1 cup flour
1 tablespoon sugar
2 teaspoons salt
½ teaspoon MSG
1¼ cups milk
1¾ cups water

filling
1 cup shredded bamboo shoots
½ pound bean sprouts, rinsed and well-drained
1½ cups shredded water chestnuts
3½ cups slivered cooked chicken
¾ cup slivered barbecued pork
¾ cup finely chopped fresh parsley
1 cup chopped fresh mushrooms
½ cup finely chopped scallion
Salt and freshly ground black pepper to taste
Oil

Beat egg slightly. Sift together dry ingredients. Mix with egg. Slowly stir in milk and water and stir until smooth.

All filling ingredients should be cut finely. Mix filling ingredients (except oil) together and sauté in a little oil for about 10 minutes, stirring occasionally. Let mixture cool. Spoon about ½ cup onto egg roll skin. Fold like an envelope. Dip in batter and fry in hot oil for about 5 minutes, turning carefully to brown both sides. Serve with Chinese mustard and/or duck sauce.

Makes approximately 2 dozen.

egg rolls

soups

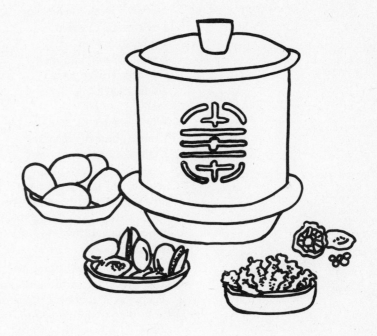

egg drop soup

4 cups chicken broth, homemade or canned
1 tablespoon cornstarch
¼ cup cold water
1 tablespoon soy sauce
Pinch of grated fresh gingerroot, or a sprinkle of
    powdered ginger
Few sprinkles freshly ground pepper
2 eggs, slightly beaten
1 tablespoon fresh parsley, coarsely chopped

garnish
A few cooked pea pods, or a small amount chopped scallions

Bring chicken broth to a boil. Dissolve cornstarch in water, stir into broth and bring to a boil again. Add soy sauce, ginger, and pepper. Holding eggs above soup, slowly pour into soup in a slow steady stream while whisking eggs into soup to form long threads. Turn off heat, add parsley, and garnish soup with pea pods or chopped scallions. If desired, warm chow mein noodles can be served with this soup.
Makes 4 servings.

soup with vegetables and meat dumplings

meat dumplings
2 slices bread
½ pound lean ground beef
Salt

White pepper
5 cups beef bouillon

soup
¼ head savoy cabbage (green cabbage can be substituted), sliced
1 leek, sliced
2 ounces fresh mushrooms, sliced
1 celery stalk, sliced
1 tablespoon oil
1 small onion, chopped
2 ounces frozen peas
4 ounces egg noodles
Salt
White pepper
1 tablespoon soy sauce
3 tablespoons sherry

Soak bread in small amount of cold water. Squeeze as dry as possible and mix with ground beef and salt and pepper to taste. Bring bouillon to a boil. Using 1 teaspoon of meat mixture, form little dumplings and drop into boiling broth. Reduce heat and simmer for 10 minutes.

For soup, slice cabbage, leek, mushrooms and celery. Heat oil in a large saucepan. Add onion and cook until golden. Add sliced vegetables and cook for 5 minutes. Remove dumplings from beef broth with a slotted spoon, drain on paper toweling and keep warm. Strain broth and add to vegetables. Add peas and noodles and simmer for 15 minutes. Return dumplings to soup. Season with salt, pepper, soy sauce and sherry. Serve immediately.

Makes 4 to 6 servings.

soup with vegetables and meat dumplings

sharks'-fin soup

¾ pound dried sharks' fins
1 tablespoon oil
2 tablespoons fresh gingerroot, sliced
¼ cup scallions, sliced
1 tablespoon sherry
3 quarts chicken broth, divided
2 tablespoons cornstarch
1 teaspoon soy sauce
¼ cup water
¼ teaspoon MSG
½ pound crab meat

Wash sharks' fins and cover with cold water. Drain, cover with fresh water and boil 3 hours. Drain, add fresh water and boil again for 3 hours. Drain and let dry. Heat oil in large saucepan. Sauté the ginger and scallions for 3 minutes. Add the sherry, 1 quart of the chicken broth and the sharks' fins. Cook over medium-high heat 15 minutes. Drain off any remaining liquid. Add the remaining broth; bring to a boil. Mix together the cornstarch, soy sauce, water, and MSG. Slowly stir into the soup. Stir in the crab meat. Heat through.

Makes approximately 8 servings.

crab soup

2 tablespoons oil
½ pound crab meat
¼ teaspoon salt
2 medium tomatoes, chopped coarsely
1½ teaspoons fresh gingerroot, chopped
5 cups chicken broth
2 eggs, beaten
1½ tablespoons vinegar
1½ tablespoons sherry
1½ tablespoons soy sauce
3 scallions, sliced

In large pot heat oil. Sauté crab meat, salt, tomatoes, and ginger for 5 minutes. Add chicken broth and cook over low heat 10 minutes. Beat eggs, and add vinegar, sherry, and soy sauce. Pour into the soup slowly. Stir in the scallions and let soup simmer for about 3 minutes.

Makes 4 to 6 servings.

oriental clam soup

2 cups chicken broth
2 cups clam juice
2 cups minced clams
1 small onion, minced
2 tablespoons fresh parsley, minced
2 tablespoons soy sauce
1 tablespoon sherry

In large saucepan combine chicken broth and clam juice. Add clams and onion and bring to a boil. Simmer for 10 minutes. Add parsley, soy sauce, and sherry and heat through.

Makes 5 to 6 servings.

chicken vegetable soup

This is delicious soup!

6 cups chicken broth
½ cup bean sprouts
¼ cup water chestnuts, thinly sliced
1 scallion, minced
½ cup bok choy, sliced (use leafy part also)
3 Chinese mushrooms, soaked and drained and sliced
½ cup snow pea pods
½ cup cooked, diced chicken
2 teaspoons soy sauce
1 tablespoon sherry
Pepper to taste

Bring chicken broth to boil in soup pot. Add vegetables and chicken and simmer about 1 minute. Add soy sauce and sherry. Add pepper to taste. If desired, cellophane noodles or very fine egg noodles may be added.

Makes 4 to 6 servings.

egg-flower soup

4 cups chicken broth
½ medium onion, chopped
½ cup celery, sliced
Pinch of salt
1 egg, beaten
½ cup chopped spinach

Place chicken broth in pot and bring to boil. Add onion, celery, and salt. Bring to boil again. Stir in beaten egg. Add spinach and let simmer for 1 minute.

Makes 4 servings.

black-mushroom soup

¼ cup dried black mushrooms
1 clove garlic, crushed
1 tablespoon sesame oil
8 cups rich chicken broth
1 piece of gingerroot, size of hazelnut
2½ tablespoons soy sauce
½ cup finely diced cooked chicken
½ cup finely diced cooked ham
½ cup diced bamboo shoots
½ cup finely chopped scallions

Soak mushrooms in warm water until soft and spongy, about 10 minutes. Squeeze out liquid and chop very fine. Crush garlic and sauté in oil for 2 or 3 seconds, remove from oil and set aside. Sauté the mushrooms in the same pan for about 5 minutes. In soup kettle bring chicken broth to boil. Add mushrooms, garlic, ginger and soy sauce. Simmer about 4 hours. Strain the broth and add chicken, ham, bamboo shoots and scallions. Simmer just to heat through the added ingredients.

Makes 8 servings.

won ton soup

dough for dumplings
4 ounces flour
Salt
1 tablespoon milk
2 tablespoons oil
1 small egg

filling
4 ounces fresh spinach, chopped
4 ounces ground pork
½ tablespoon soy souce
⅛ teaspoon powdered ginger

soup
5 cups chicken broth
2 tablespoons chopped chives

In bowl, stir together flour and salt. Add milk, oil and egg. Knead dough until it is smooth. On a floured board roll out dough until it is paper thin. Cut into 3-inch squares. Cover with a kitchen towel while you prepare filling.

Thoroughly wash spinach; remove coarse stems. Place in bowl and barely cover with boiling water; let stand for 3 minutes. Drain well and coarsely chop. Add ground pork, soy sauce and ginger. Blend thoroughly. Place 1 teaspoon of filling on each dough square, giving filling a lengthy shape. Fold over dough from one side and roll up jelly-roll fashion. Press ends of roll together to seal.

Bring chicken broth to a boil. Add won tons and simmer over low heat for 20 minutes. Spoon soup into bowls. Garnish with chopped chives.

Makes 6 servings.

celery soup

1 heaping tablespoon dried Chinese mushrooms
½ pound pork shoulder
2 small onions, minced
1 clove garlic, minced
2 small celeriac roots with green tops (celery stalks
   may be substituted)
4 tablespoons oil
3 cups hot chicken broth
1 ounce transparent noodles
2 tablespoons soy sauce
⅛ teaspoon powdered ginger

Soak Chinese mushrooms in cold water for 30 minutes. Cut pork into 1½-inch long, ½-inch-thick strips. Mince onions and garlic. Cut off celery tops and set aside. Brush celeriac roots under running cold water, peel and cut into ½-inch cubes. Heat oil in saucepan. Add pork and brown on all sides while stirring constantly for about 3 minutes. Add onions, garlic and celeriac root and cook for 5 minutes more. Drain mushrooms and cut in halves or quarter if very large, and also add to saucepan. Pour in chicken broth, cover and simmer over low heat for 25 minutes. Meanwhile, in another saucepan, bring salted water to a boil, add noodles, remove from heat immediately and let stand for 5 minutes. Drain noodles. Five minutes before end of cooking time of soup, add coarsely chopped celery leaves. Season to taste with soy sauce and ginger.

Place noodles in soup tureen or 4 individual Chinese soup bowls, pour soup over noodles and serve.

Makes 4 servings.

eggs

egg foo yong

Oil to cover bottom of skillet
½ pound fresh mushrooms, sliced
½ cup chopped celery
½ cup diced scallions
1 cup fresh bean sprouts, rinsed and drained
1 cup leftover cooked chicken, beef, or shrimp, cut into small pieces
4 eggs
Salt and pepper to taste

Sauté mushrooms, celery, and scallions for 5 minutes. Cool. Add bean sprouts and chicken, beef, or shrimp to sautéed mixture. In large bowl beat eggs well with salt and pepper. Combine other ingredients with eggs. Drop by spoonfuls into greased skillet. Cook over medium-high heat until browned on both sides. You may use a wok, and drop mixture by spoonfuls just to cover bottom of wok.

Makes 2 servings as main course or 4 servings as appetizer.

simple egg foo yong

These are simple and delicious. Leftover chicken, beef, shrimp, etc., may also be added to rest of ingredients.

Oil for cooking
½ cup celery, thinly sliced diagonally
½ cup diced scallions
½ cup sliced fresh mushrooms
4 eggs
Salt and pepper to taste
1 cup fresh bean sprouts

Heat oil in skillet (or wok, preferably), and sauté celery for 2 minutes. Add scallions and mushrooms and sauté another minute. Remove vegetables from skillet. Beat eggs in bowl with seasonings and add sautéed vegetables and bean sprouts. Add more oil to skillet or wok, if necessary, and add egg mixture to skillet by spoonfuls, or, if cooking in wok, add enough egg mixture just to cover bottom of wok. Cook over medium-high heat until brown, turn and brown other side. Serve with duck sauce.

Makes 2 servings as a main course or 4 servings as an appetizer.

scrambled eggs with shrimp

½ pound shrimp, cooked
1 teaspoon rice wine or sherry
½ teaspoon cornstarch
Salt (about ½ teaspoon)
2 tablespoons oil
6 eggs, beaten lightly
Salt to taste

Marinate shrimp in mixture of wine or sherry, cornstarch, and salt for 15 minutes. Heat oil in large skillet and sauté shrimp over medium-high heat for approximately 2 minutes. Remove from skillet. Add salt to taste to beaten eggs and add shrimps to egg mixture. Add more oil if necessary to skillet, heat to medium-high, pour in egg–shrimp mixture and cook and stir until done to taste.
Makes 3 to 4 servings.

unusual scrambled eggs

4 eggs
½ teaspoon salt
Freshly ground black pepper to taste
Dash of monosodium glutamate (MSG) (optional)
½ cup finely chopped green pepper
Oil for cooking, enough to cover bottom of pan

Beat eggs with salt and pepper and MSG. Add green pepper. Heat oil in skillet and cook mixture over medium-high heat until desired doneness. (Don't cook until dry.)
Makes 2 servings.

meat

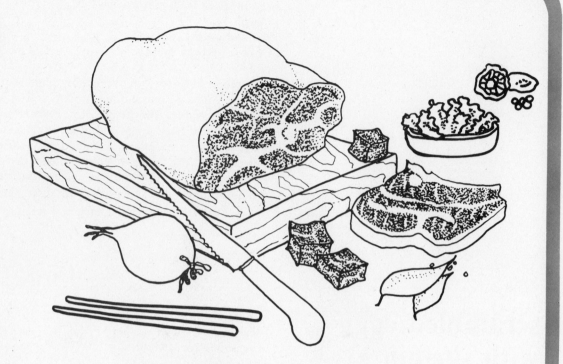

oriental pepper steak

1 pound round steak
¼ cup oil
½ teaspoon salt
Pepper to taste
½ cup chopped scallion
2 cloves garlic, finely chopped
4 green peppers, cut into bite-size pieces
1 cup sliced celery
1½ cups beef bouillon
2 tablespoons cornstarch
¼ cup cold water
1 tablespoon soy sauce
Cooked rice

Cut steak into thin slices and then into 2-inch pieces. To make slicing easier, partially freeze the meat. Heat oil in large skillet. Add salt and pepper. Cook meat over medium to high heat until brown, stirring frequently. Add scallion and garlic. Add green peppers and celery and stir. Add bouillon, cover and cook until vegetables are tender but still crisp. Do not overcook. Meanwhile, combine cornstarch and water. Blend in soy sauce until it makes a smooth paste. Slowly add to meat mixture, stirring constantly until liquid is thickened. Serve with rice.

Makes 4 servings.

chinese stir-fried beef and mushrooms

chinese stir-fried beef and mushrooms

½ pound dried Chinese mushrooms
3 pounds lean steak, cut into thin strips
¼ cup flour
1 tablespoon sugar
½ cup sherry
½ cup soy sauce
¾ cup oil, divided
1 2-inch slice fresh gingerroot, minced
1 cup onions, chopped
2 cups beef bouillon
Salt to taste

Soak the mushrooms in water for 30 minutes. Drain well and set aside. Cut the steak into strips. In a bowl combine flour, sugar, sherry and soy sauce. Add the beef and marinate for 30 minutes, stirring frequently. Heat ½ cup of the oil in a wok. Stir-fry the gingerroot for 1 minute. Add the beef with the marinade and stir-fry until the beef changes color. Remove the beef from the wok. Add the remaining oil to wok. Add the onions and stir-fry until almost tender. Add mushrooms and stir-fry until soft. Place the beef in the wok and stir-fry for about 2 minutes. Add the bouillon, bring to a boil and reduce heat. Add salt, cover and cook for 2 minutes.

Makes 6 to 8 servings.

21

ginger beef

ginger beef

1 cup onions, minced
2 cloves of garlic, pressed
2 teaspoons turmeric
2 teaspoons ginger
1 teaspoon chili powder
1 teaspoon salt
3 pounds of lean beef, cut into cubes
8 fresh tomatoes, peeled and cut into large pieces
½ cup peanut oil
4 cups beef bouillon
Boiled rice
Strips of red sweet pepper for garnish

Combine onions, garlic, turmeric, ginger, chili powder and salt in
bowl. Mix well. Prepare the beef and place in shallow dish.
Sprinkle with the onion–garlic mixture and refrigerate for 3 hours,
stirring occasionally. Prepare tomatoes. In large skillet heat oil.
Stir-fry the beef until browned on all sides. Place beef in casserole
and add skillet drippings, tomatoes and bouillon. Bake, covered, in
a 325°F oven for about 2 hours or until the beef is tender. Serve
with boiled rice and garnish with strips of red sweet pepper.
Makes 6 to 8 servings.

22

beef with spinach

½ pound beef, thinly sliced

marinade
2 tablespoons rice wine or sherry
½ teaspoon salt
Freshly ground black pepper to taste
1 egg white
1 tablespoon chopped leek (onion may be substituted)
½ teaspoon grated gingerroot
1 teaspoon chili powder
1 teaspoon grated garlic
1 tablespoon cornstarch

Oil for cooking
1 tablespoon soy sauce
1 teaspoon vinegar
1¼ teaspoons sugar, divided
1 package (10 ounces) spinach, washed and torn into bite-size pieces
Salt to taste

Cut beef into bite-size pieces. Mix marinade ingredients and marinate beef for 30 minutes. Heat oil in skillet or wok and sauté beef over medium-high heat for approximately 3 to 4 minutes. Add soy sauce, vinegar and 1 teaspoon sugar. Stir well and remove meat mixture to serving platter. Heat more oil if necessary and sauté spinach over high heat just until tender, 1 to 2 minutes. Add salt to taste and ¼ teaspoon sugar, and place on serving platter with beef.
Makes 2 servings.

tomato beef

2 tablespoons cornstarch
1 tablespoon soy sauce
1 tablespoon brandy
½ pound flank steak, sliced ⅛ inch thick
2 tablespoons peanut oil
¼ cup chopped onion
¼ cup sliced celery (sliced diagonally)
1 small green pepper, cut into 1-inch squares
2 tomatoes, each cut into 8 sections
¼ cup sliced water chestnuts
1 cup chicken broth, heated
1½ teaspoons catsup
½ (scant) teaspoon salt
1 teaspoon sugar
1 tablespoon cornstarch mixed with about
  3 tablespoons cold water

Mix together cornstarch, soy sauce, and brandy. Place sliced flank steak in mixture and marinate about 15 minutes. Heat oil in wok or pan. Add steak and stir-fry until golden brown. Remove from pan and set aside. Sauté onion and celery for about 20 seconds, then add green pepper, tomatoes, and water chestnuts. Toss several times. Add broth, cover and let steam for 1 minute. Remove cover, add beef and mix well. Cover and steam for about 20 seconds. Add catsup, salt, and sugar; mix well. Thicken with cornstarch mixture. Don't let the sauce get too thick.
Makes 2 to 3 servings.

sandie's beef oriental

½ pound lean, tender beef, cut into strips
2 tablespoons peanut oil
1 clove garlic, chopped
1 onion, chopped
2 cups frozen green beans, French-style
1 cup celery, sliced
1 tablespoon cornstarch
1 tablespoon soy sauce
¾ cup liquid (1 tablespoon sherry, juice from canned mushrooms and water, or 1 tablespoon sherry and beef bouillon)
1 can sliced mushrooms, or 1 cup fresh mushrooms, sliced
Strips of pimiento for garnish
Cooked rice

Brown beef in oil, to which garlic is added. Add onion, beans, and celery. Cook 4 to 6 minutes, stirring frequently. Combine cornstarch and soy sauce with liquid. Add to meat mixture with mushrooms. Stir, cooking until liquid is glossy. Cover and cook until beans are tender but crisp. Garnish with pimiento and serve with rice.

Makes 4 servings.

beef with snow peas

½ pound beef, thinly sliced

marinade
1 teaspoon cornstarch
1 teaspoon soy sauce
2 teaspoons sherry
¼ teaspoon sugar
¼ teaspoon oil

½ pound snow peas, with strings removed
2 teaspoons cornstarch mixed with 2 teaspoons cold water
⅛ teaspoon freshly ground black pepper
½ teaspoon sugar
¼ teaspoon MSG
2 tablespoons oil, divided
¼ teaspoon salt
1 teaspoon grated fresh gingerroot
½ cup chicken stock

Slice beef and set aside.

Mix marinade ingredients and marinate beef while preparing rest of ingredients.

String snow peas. Mix together cornstarch and water. Add pepper, sugar, and MSG. Heat skillet or wok to medium-high. Add 1 tablespoon oil, salt, and gingerroot. Add snow peas, stir, and add the chicken stock. Cover for 10 seconds. Uncover, stir, and remove from pan. Reheat pan and add remaining 1 tablespoon oil. When pan is hot, add beef and stir-fry only about 45 seconds, until beef is almost cooked. Then add snow peas and cornstarch mixture. Stir until sauce is thickened.

Makes 2 to 3 servings.

oriental beef with vegetables

½ pound thinly sliced beef
½ cup thinly sliced carrots, cut at an angle
2 cloves garlic, crushed
2 tablespoons soy sauce
3 tablespoons sherry
2 tablespoons oil
4 scallions, cut into ½-inch pieces
½ cup thinly sliced celery, cut at an angle
½ teaspoon powdered mustard
1 pound fresh spinach, chopped

Marinate beef, carrots and garlic in a mixture of soy sauce and sherry, for at least 6 hours. Heat oil in wok. Remove meat from marinade and stir-fry for 1 minute. Add remaining ingredients and stir-fry only until vegetables are very bright in color, approximately 2 to 3 minutes. Serve with rice, if desired.

Makes 3 to 4 servings.

unusual beef

marinade
1 tablespoon sherry
2 tablespoons soy sauce
1 teaspoon cornstarch

½ pound lean beef, sliced and cut into bite-size pieces
4 tablespoons oil
3 cups potato chips
1 cup snow peas, tips broken off
Sprinkles of sherry

Blend marinade ingredients and marinate beef in mixture for 15 minutes. Heat oil to medium-high heat and stir-fry beef just until color changes. Add potato chips and snow peas and stir just until heated through, about 30 seconds. Sprinkle with sherry to taste and serve immediately.

Makes 2 servings.

marinated flank steak

1 flank steak, approximately 2 pounds

marinade
4 tablespoons lemon juice
¼ cup soy sauce
3 tablespoons honey
3 scallions, finely chopped
2 tablespoons sesame oil

Score steak on each side. Combine marinade ingredients and place steak in mixture and refrigerate overnight, turning occasionally. Broil steak on preheated broiler pan about 4 minutes on each side, basting frequently with marinade. Cut steak on angle into very thin slices.

Makes 2 to 3 servings.

chinese liver

Delicious with rice.

1 pound beef liver
2½ tablespoons flour
5 tablespoons safflower oil
Salt to taste
Pepper to taste
3 tablespoons soy sauce
2 tablespoons sherry
2 large onions, thinly sliced
1 cup beef bouillon
1 red pepper, cut into strips
1 green pepper, cut into strips
½ pound savoy cabbage, cut into strips
½ pound fresh bean sprouts
1 small can bamboo shoots

Pat liver dry with paper toweling and cut into thin slices. Coat with flour. Heat oil in skillet, add liver and brown on all sides. Remove and season to taste with salt and pepper. Set aside and keep warm. Add soy sauce and sherry to pan drippings, as well as onion. Simmer for 5 minutes. Pour in beef bouillon. Add green and red peppers and cabbage. Simmer for 10 minutes. Vegetables should still be crunchy. Add bean sprouts, bamboo shoots and liver. Heat through and serve.

Makes approximately 3 servings.

apricot tongue

1 beef tongue
Water
¼ cup soy sauce
2 cloves garlic, cut

sauce
⅔ cup brown sugar
¾ cup catsup
¼ teaspoon fresh gingerroot, grated, or ½ teaspoon powdered ginger
1 tablespoon soy sauce
1 package dried apricots

Place tongue in large pot. Add water to cover. Mix in ¼ cup soy sauce and garlic. Bring to boil and simmer until tongue is tender.

To make sauce, combine all ingredients in saucepan and simmer slowly until apricots are soft. Pour sauce over sliced tongue.

Makes 4 servings.

beef slices peking

beef slices peking

marinade
3 tablespoons soy sauce
1 tablespoon sherry

1 pound lean beef, sliced
    paper thin
1 cup oil
2 tablespoons flour

2 leeks, thinly sliced
2 garlic cloves, minced
½ teaspoon powdered ginger
2 tablespoons soy sauce
⅛ teaspoon ground anise
½ cup beef broth
1 teaspoon cornstarch

In a deep bowl blend soy sauce and sherry. Add beef slices, coat well, cover and let stand for 1 hour. Heat oil in a large skillet. Thoroughly drain beef slices on paper toweling. Sprinkle with flour, add to hot oil and deep-fry for 3 minutes. Remove meat slices with slotted spoon, drain, set aside and keep warm. Take 4 tablespoons of hot oil and pour into another skillet. Throw away rest of frying oil. Reheat oil, add leeks and garlic. Cook for 5 minutes while stirring. Add meat slices. Season with powdered ginger, soy sauce and anise. Pour in beef broth. Cover and simmer over very low heat for 1 hour. At end of cooking time, bring to a quick boil. Blend cornstarch with small amount of cold water, add to skillet, stirring constantly until sauce is slightly thickened and bubbly. Correct seasoning, if necessary, and serve immediately.

Makes 2 servings.

chinese fondue

chicken bouillon
6 cups chicken stock
2 medium carrots, thinly sliced
1 leek, finely sliced
1 stalk celery, thinly sliced
2 tablespoons parsley,
  coarsely chopped

sauce tartare
5 tablespoons mayonnaise
2 tablespoons capers
2 tablespoons chopped chives
2 dill pickles, finely chopped
2 teaspoons lemon juice
2 tablespoons evaporated milk
Salt
Pinch of sugar
White pepper

catsup sauce
5 tablespoons mayonnaise
2 tablespoons catsup
1 teaspoon Worchestershire sauce
1 teaspoon curry powder
Pinch of sugar
Salt

2 pounds lean beef, cut into
  thin slices
2 cups boiling water

Pour chicken stock in fondue pot and place on top of stove. Add carrots, leek, celery and parsley. Let simmer for 20 minutes. Meanwhile prepare sauces.

For Tartare Sauce, blend mayonnaise, capers, chives, dill pickles, lemon juice and evaporated milk. Season to taste with salt, sugar and white pepper.

To prepare Catsup Sauce, stir together thoroughly mayonnaise, catsup, Worchestershire sauce, and curry powder. Season to taste with sugar and salt.

Pat meat dry with paper toweling. Cut into thin slices. Place fondue pot with chicken bouillon on burner in middle of table. Make sure that broth continues to simmer. Since broth will evaporate, repldnish it from time to time with boiling, hot water. Fondue is eaten in following fashion: Roll up slice of beef, place on fondue fork and let cook in chicken broth to desired doneness. Dunk in sauce—when all the beef slices have been cooked, broth is ladled into bowls and eaten too.

Makes approximately 4 servings.

chinese fondue

marinated steak slices

marinated steak slices

1¼ pounds fillet steak, or sirloin

marinade
4 tablespoons sherry
4 tablespoons soy sauce
1½ heaping tablespoons cornstarch
Salt to taste
Pinch of sugar
Pinch of white pepper

4 tablespoons oil

Cut beef into thin slices. Prepare marinade by blending thoroughly the sherry, soy sauce and cornstarch. Season with salt, sugar and white pepper. Pour marinade over meat slices and let marinate for 1 hour. In large skillet heat oil until very hot. Pour in meat with marinade and cook for 5 minutes. Spoon into preheated bowl and serve with rice.

Makes 2 to 3 servings.

beef and rice oriental

1¼ cups cooked rice
1 pound ground beef
2 medium onions, sliced
2 cups fresh bean sprouts
1 package frozen cut green beans
1 cup beef bouillon
⅓ cup soy sauce
½ cup water
½ teaspoon powdered ginger

Preheat oven to 425°F. Mix all ingredients together in casserole dish. Bake covered for about 40 minutes.
Makes 4 servings.

beef sukiyaki

My family enjoys this recipe very much. Have everything ready before you start cooking. This meal is fun to prepare in a wok in front of guests.

2 pounds beef sirloin, cut into strips
1 large Bermuda onion
3 stalks celery
¼ pound fresh mushrooms
12 scallions
8 ounces canned water chestnuts
¼ pound fresh spinach
1 tablespoon oil
¾ cup beef bouillon
½ cup soy sauce
¼ cup vermouth
1 tablespoon sugar

Have the butcher cut the sirloin into thin strips, or, if you are cutting it, partially freeze it to make it easier to slice. Slice onion and put aside. Slice the celery at an angle into thin slices. Set aside. Thinly slice mushrooms and set aside. Slice scallions into approximately 1½-inch pieces. Drain the water chestnuts and slice in half. Wash spinach and tear into pieces. Arrange meat and vegetables on large platter. Put oil into extra-large skillet or wok. Brown the meat and push to side of pan or wok. Add all vegetables except spinach and stir in bouillon, soy sauce, vermouth and sugar. Let sizzle for 5 minutes. Add spinach, cover and cook 2 minutes more. Serve with rice.
Makes 3 to 4 servings.

braised beef

2 tablespoons oil
2 pounds cubed beef
2 tablespoons sherry
1¼ cups water
½ cup soy sauce
½-inch piece of gingerroot, crushed
3 cloves star anise
1 tablespoon brown sugar
4 hard-boiled eggs, shelled

Heat oil in deep pot and brown beef over medium-high heat. Add sherry, water, soy sauce, gingerroot, and star anise, and bring to a boil. Reduce heat and simmer 1 hour. Add brown sugar and eggs and continue cooking for 20 minutes, or until beef is tender. Remove eggs, halve, and place on serving platter with beef.
Makes 4 servings.

beef in oyster sauce

1 pound lean beef, cut into bite-size pieces
2 tablespoons soy sauce
1 tablespoon rice wine or sherry
1 teaspoon cornstarch
Oil for cooking
1 teaspoon sugar, more or less, to taste
3 tablespoons oyster sauce
Cooked rice

Marinate beef in mixture of soy sauce, wine or sherry, and cornstarch for 30 minutes. Heat oil in skillet or wok to medium-high heat. Add beef and stir-fry until done, approximately 3 to 4 minutes. Add sugar and oyster sauce and mix well. Serve with rice.
Makes 2 to 3 servings.

31

oriental meat balls

These are very tasty meatballs.

2 pounds lean ground beef
2½ teaspoons salt, divided
⅛ teaspoon freshly ground black pepper
1 egg, beaten
2 tablespoons flour
Small amount freshly ground black pepper
½ cup oil
12 ounces canned chicken broth
3 tablespoons cornstarch
2 to 3 teaspoons soy sauce
½ cup vinegar
½ cup light corn syrup
5 medium green peppers, cut in sixths
8 slices canned pineapple, quartered, or chunks or tidbits
10 maraschino cherries (optional)

Combine beef, 1 teaspoon salt, and ⅛ teaspoon pepper. Shape into small meatballs. Combine egg, flour, ½ teaspoon salt, and a small amount of pepper. Beat until smooth. In large frying pan heat oil and remaining 1 teaspoon salt. Gently place meatballs in batter, one or two at a time, and fry in the hot oil, browning well on all sides. Remove meatballs from pan. Drain off remaining oil. Blend ½ cup of the chicken broth with cornstarch. Add remaining chicken broth, soy sauce, vinegar, and corn syrup and cook over medium heat, stirring constantly, until thick and clear. Add green peppers, pineapple, and cherries. Lower heat and cook slowly for about 10 minutes. Pour over meatballs. Serve with rice.
Makes 6 servings.

wok surprise

Oil for cooking
1 cup sliced green pepper
1 cup celery, sliced diagonally
1 cup sliced zucchini
2 cups leftover cooked roast beef, thinly sliced
Beef gravy, beef broth, or chicken broth
½ cup fresh mushrooms, sliced
2 cups fresh bean sprouts
2 cups fresh spinach, torn into bite-size pieces
Freshly ground black pepper to taste
Soy sauce to taste
Cornstarch mixed with cold water

Put small amount of oil in wok and heat to medium-high. Add green pepper and celery. Stir-fry for 1 minute. Add zucchini and stir-fry for 2 more minutes, or until the vegetables are bright in color and still crisp. Push vegetables up sides of wok (or remove) and place roast beef and a little gravy or beef broth, or chicken broth in wok, and toss meat until hot. Push meat up sides of wok and place mushrooms and bean sprouts in wok and stir-fry for 1 minute. Add previously cooked vegetables, beef, spinach, pepper and soy sauce. If desired, you may add a little cornstarch mixed with cold water to thicken the gravy. Serve with rice, if desired.
Makes 4 servings.

meatballs chinese-style

meatballs
2 pounds ground beef
1 egg
2 tablespoons onion, chopped
1 tablespoon cornstarch
1 teaspoon salt
Freshly ground black pepper to taste
Peanut oil

sauce
1 cup pineapple juice
1 tablespoon oil
3 tablespoons cornstarch
1 tablespoon soy sauce
3 tablespoons vinegar
6 tablespoons water
½ cup sugar
1 green pepper, cut into small chunks
1 small can pineapple chunks, drained

Combine all ingredients for meatballs and shape into 1 inch-balls. Brown in small amount of peanut oil. Drain.

In large saucepan combine pineapple juice and oil. Set aside. Mix together cornstarch, soy sauce, vinegar, water, and sugar. Add to pineapple juice and oil. Bring to boil, and simmer 1 minute. Add green pepper and pineapple chunks. Add meatballs.

Makes approximately 50 meatballs.

unusual hamburgers

1 pound ground beef
1 egg, beaten
¼ cup finely chopped water chestnuts
2 tablespoons minced onions
3 tablespoons minced mushrooms
½ teaspoon MSG
⅛ teaspoon freshly ground black pepper
1 tablespoon oyster sauce

Mix ground beef with remaining ingredients. Shape into two patties, about ¾ inch thick. Broil about 4 inches from heat, for about 5 minutes. Turn and broil other side 4 to 5 minutes.

Makes 2 servings.

chinese hamburgers

2 pounds ground meat, lean
2 tablespoons soy sauce
1 medium onion, finely chopped
1 medium green pepper, finely chopped
4 water chestnuts, finely chopped
¼ teaspoon MSG
Salt to taste
Pepper to taste
2 eggs, lightly beaten

Combine all ingredients and mix thoroughly. Form into patties and broil in oven or cook on hibachi or grill, approximately 5 minutes on each side.

Makes 8 patties.

sweet-and-sour pork

1½ pounds lean pork, cut in 1-inch cubes
3 tablespoons soy sauce
3 tablespoons dry white wine
2 carrots, cut into thin strips
1 red sweet pepper, seeds removed, and cut into thin rings
4 tablespoons olive oil, divided
1 small slice fresh gingerroot, minced
½ cup onions, chopped
¼ pound fresh mushrooms, sliced
½ cup beef broth
1 recipe Chinese Sweet-and-Sour Sauce (see Index)
Boiled rice

Place the pork in a shallow dish. Combine soy sauce and wine and pour over the pork. Turn to coat all sides. Marinate for about 20 to 30 minutes, stirring frequently. Cut the carrots and set aside. Cut pepper into rings and set aside.

Heat 2 tablespoons of the oil in a wok and add the gingerroot. Place the pork in the wok and stir-fry for about 5 minutes. Remove the pork and set aside. Add remaining oil to wok. Add carrots, sweet pepper, onions and mushrooms and stir-fry for about 5 minutes or until the carrots and sweet pepper are tender but still on the crisp side. Add the pork and stir-fry for 5 minutes longer. Add broth and mix well. Stir in the Sweet-and-Sour Sauce and bring to a boil. Reduce heat to low, cover wok and cook for 2 minutes longer. Serve with rice.

Makes 4 servings.

chinese spareribs with fresh peppers

4 pounds spareribs, cut into serving pieces
Salt to taste
⅔ cup brown sugar
3 tablespoons cornstarch
1 teaspoon powdered ginger
1 teaspoon powdered mustard
2 cups fresh orange juice
⅓ cup fresh lemon juice
⅓ cup soy sauce
3 tablespoons butter or margarine
½ pound fresh mushrooms, sliced if large
1 medium onion, chopped
1 green sweet pepper, cut into squares
1 red sweet pepper, cut into squares
1 large can pineapple chunks

Cut the spareribs into serving pieces. Place in roasting pan bone-side-down and sprinkle with salt to taste. Bake in a 350°F oven for 1 hour. Drain off excess fat. In saucepan combine brown sugar, cornstarch, ginger, and mustard. Stir in orange juice, lemon juice, and soy sauce. Bring to a boil and cook and stir until thickened. Set aside. Melt the butter or margarine in skillet. Sauté mushrooms for 5 minutes. Pour sauce over spareribs. Add the onion, green and red peppers, pineapple, and mushrooms. Bake for 30 minutes, basting occasionally.

Makes 4 to 5 servings.

sweet-and-sour pork
lime spareribs

lime spareribs

These are very good!

4 pounds spareribs, cut into serving pieces
¼ cup olive oil
1 cup onions, chopped
1 cup fresh mushrooms, sliced
1 clove garlic, minced
½ cup chili sauce
2 tablespoons red wine vinegar
¼ cup lime juice
2 tablespoons prepared mustard
¼ cup soy sauce
⅔ cup water
2 tablespoons honey
1 teaspoon salt
Freshly ground pepper to taste

Cut spareribs into serving pieces and place in baking pan. Heat oil in saucepan. Sauté onions, mushrooms and garlic, until tender. Add chili sauce, vinegar, lime juice, mustard, soy sauce, water, honey, salt and pepper, and mix thoroughly. Pour sauce over the spareribs. Bake in a 325°F oven for 1 hour, or until the spareribs are tender. Baste frequently.

Makes 6 to 8 servings.

chinese pork with peas

12 ounces lean pork

marinade
2 tablespoons soy sauce
2 teaspoons sherry
⅛ teaspoon MSG
1 egg white
1 teaspoon cornstarch
Salt
White pepper

4 ounces frozen peas
8 tablespoons oil, divided
½ cup hot beef broth
Salt

Sugar
1 leek, cut into julienne strips
1 clove garlic, minced
1 4-ounce can sliced mushrooms
1 4-ounce can bamboo shoots
1 preserved ginger, sliced
1 tablespoon sherry
1 tablespoon cornstarch
2 teaspoons soy sauce
2 tablespoons oyster sauce
Salt
White pepper
Pinch of powdered ginger
Sugar

Cut meat crosswise into thin strips.

Prepare marinade by combining and blending soy sauce, sherry, MSG, egg white and cornstarch. Season to taste with salt and white pepper. Pour over pork strips, cover and let marinate for 30 minutes.

Meanwhile, thaw peas. Heat 2 tablespoons of the oil in a small saucepan. Add peas and pour in beef broth. Season to taste with salt and sugar, and cook for 5 minutes. Drain peas, reserving cooking liquid, and keep warm. Heat 3 tablespoons of the oil in a large saucepan. Add leek, garlic, mushrooms, bamboo shoots and ginger. Cook for 5 minutes, stirring constantly. Set aside and keep warm. Heat rest of oil (3 tablespoons) in skillet. Add meat together with marinade and cook for 3 minutes or until meat is browned, stirring occasionally. Add meat and peas to large saucepan with vegetables. Pour in sherry and reserved cooking liquid and bring to a boil. Blend cornstarch with soy sauce and oyster sauce and stir in until slightly thickened and bubbly. Season to taste with salt, pepper, ginger and sugar. Serve immediately.

Makes 2 to 3 servings.

chinese pork with peas

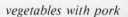
vegetables with pork

vegetables with pork

¼ **cup butter**
4 cups celery, sliced diagonally
1 green sweet pepper, sliced
1 red sweet pepper, sliced
½ **pound fresh mushrooms, sliced**
½ **cup onions, sliced**
2 cups cubed cooked pork
1¼ **cups beef bouillon**
1 tablespoon cornstarch
3 tablespoons soy sauce
½ **teaspoon powdered ginger**
¼ **teaspoon salt**
Freshly ground pepper to taste
Boiled rice

Melt butter in a wok. Add celery and stir-fry for 5 minutes. Stir in the green and red pepper, mushrooms, and onions and stir-fry for another 5 minutes. Stir in the pork and beef bouillon and bring to a boil. Reduce heat and simmer for 5 minutes. Blend the cornstarch with the soy sauce, ginger, salt, and pepper. Stir into the pork mixture. Cook, stirring constantly, just until heated through and thickened. Serve over rice.

Makes 6 servings.

chop suey

cantonese pork roast

2½ to 3 pounds boneless pork roast
1 tablespoon soy sauce
2 tablespoons chicken broth
1 tablespoon honey
1 tablespoon sugar
Salt to taste
2 tablespoons sesame-seed oil

Rinse pork and pat dry with paper toweling. Blend next five ingredients and spoon over meat and rub in thoroughly. Place roast in bowl, cover and let stand for 1 hour. Remove and drain, reserving any marinade. Brush meat with oil and place in ovenproof dish. Brush with reserved marinade. Place in preheated 325°F oven and roast for approximately 1½ hours.
Makes 4 to 6 servings.

chop suey

1 pound lean pork, cut into thin slices
2 tablespoons sherry
2 tablespoons soy sauce
Salt to taste
Freshly ground pepper to taste
Pinch of powdered ginger
2 ounces transparent noodles, broken into small pieces
1 stalk celery, cut into thin slices
4 tablespoons dried Chinese mushrooms, soaked in water for
  30 minutes
8 tablespoons oil
2 medium onions, thinly sliced
¼ cup bamboo shoots, thinly sliced
1 cup fresh bean sprouts
½ pound fresh mushrooms, sliced
3 tablespoons soy sauce
1 teaspoon sugar
⅛ teaspoon MSG
1 tablespoon cornstarch
2 jiggers sherry
Cooked rice

Cut pork into thin slices and mix with 2 tablespoons sherry, 2 tablespoons soy sauce, salt, pepper, and ginger. Place in glass or ceramic bowl. Press down meat and cover. Let marinate for 1 hour. Break noodles into small pieces and boil in salted water for 5 minutes. Drain and set aside. Cut celery in thin slices; blanch for 5 minutes. Drain and set aside. Slice Chinese mushrooms into bite-size pieces.

Heat oil in skillet until very hot. Add marinated pork and fry for 2 minutes. Remove and keep warm. Add onions, bamboo shoots, bean sprouts, and fresh mushrooms. Simmer for 3 minutes. Fold in meat, celery, and noodles. Season with 3 tablespoons soy sauce, sugar, and MSG. Stirring carefully, cook for an additional 3 minutes. Blend cornstarch with 2 jiggers sherry and slowly stir into sauce until sauce is thick and bubbly. Correct seasonings if necessary and serve immediately with rice.

Makes approximately 3 servings.

poultry

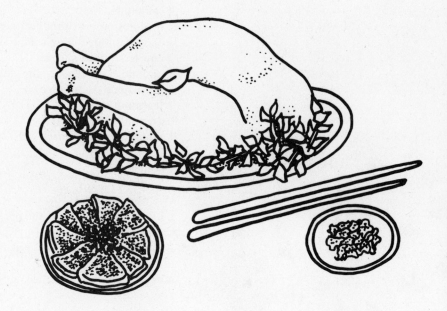

oriental chicken

⅓ cup flour
¼ teaspoon nutmeg
¼ teaspoon grated gingerroot
2 chickens, cut up
Oil for cooking
1 can sliced pineapple, 20 ounces; drain and reserve juice
¼ cup soy sauce
2 tablespoons sugar
2 cloves garlic, crushed
Rice

Blend flour, nutmeg, and gingerroot. Coat chicken with this mixture and brown well in oil in skillet. Transfer chicken to casserole dish and cover with sauce made from pineapple juice, soy sauce, sugar, and garlic. Bake, lightly covered, at 350°F for 1 hour. Brown pineapple slices in skillet and arrange on serving platter with chicken. Serve with rice.

Makes approximately 6 servings.

peking duck

These are very, very delicious.

4 to 5 pound duck
6 cups water
¼ cup honey
4 slices of fresh gingerroot, about 1 inch in diameter and
  ⅛ inch thick
2 scallions, sliced

sauce
¼ cup hoisin sauce
1 tablespoon water
1 teaspoon sesame-seed oil
2 teaspoons sugar

12 scallion brushes
Mandarin Pancakes (see Index)

Wash the duck thoroughly with cold water, and dry. Tie a cord tightly around the neck skin and suspend the duck in an airy place to dry the skin (about 3 hours). Bring water to boil. Add honey, gingerroot, and sliced scallions. Lower the duck by its string into the boiling liquid and moisten the duck's skin thoroughly, using a spoon. Suspend the duck by its cord until it is dry (about 3 hours).

Make the sauce by combining all the sauce ingredients in a small pan; stir until the sugar dissolves. Bring to a boil. Then simmer for 3 minutes. Set aside to cool. Cut scallions to 3-inch lengths and trim off roots. Stand each scallion on end and make 4 intersecting cuts 1 inch deep into its stalk. Repeat at other end. Place scallions in ice water and refrigerate until cut parts curl. Preheat oven to 375°F.

Untie the duck and cut off any loose neck skin. Place duck, breast-side-up, on a rack and set in a roasting pan. Roast for 1 hour. Lower heat to 300°F, turn the duck on its breast, and roast for 30 minutes longer. Raise the heat to 375°F, return the duck to its back, and roast for 30 minutes. Transfer to carving board.

With a small, sharp knife and using your fingers, remove the crisp skin from the breast, sides, and back of duck. Cut the skin into 2-by 3-inch rectangles and arrange them in a single layer on a platter. Cut the wings and drumsticks from the duck, and cut all the meat away from the breast and carcass. Slice the meat into pieces 2½ inches long and ½ inch wide, and arrange them on another platter.

Serve the duck with Mandarin pancakes, sauce, and the scallion brushes. Dip a scallion brush into the sauce and brush a pancake with it. The scallion is placed in the middle of the pancake with a piece of duck skin and a piece of meat. The pancake is rolled around the pieces and eaten like a sandwich.

Makes approximately 6 servings.

pineapple duck

1 duck, about 4 pounds
4 slices canned pineapple
1 large green pepper, cut into 1-inch squares
2 tablespoons oil
1 teaspoon salt
¼ teaspoon pepper
½ teaspoon MSG
1 tablespoon soy sauce
1 tablespoon cornstarch mixed with 2 tablespoons cold water

Clean and quarter duck. Cover with boiling water and simmer gently until tender. Remove from broth and let duck drain. Reserve broth. Cut each slice of pineapple into 8 pieces. Cut pepper into squares. Preheat skillet and add oil. Place pieces of duck in skillet, along with salt and pepper. Brown gently, turning frequently. When browned, add the pineapple and green pepper and stir-fry a few seconds. Add the broth, MSG, and soy sauce. Cover and simmer about 10 minutes. Thicken slightly with cornstarch mixture. Serve with rice.

Makes 3 servings.

mandarin pancakes

These are traditionally served with Peking Duck (see Index). Or, as a shortcut, you may use leftover duck that has a crisp skin. These are really very easy to make!

2 cups sifted all-purpose flour
¾ cup boiling water
1 to 2 tablespoons sesame-seed oil

Make a well in the sifted flour in bowl and pour the water into it. Mix with a wooden spoon until it is a soft dough. Knead the dough gently on a lightly floured surface for 10 minutes. It should be smooth. Let it rest under a damp kitchen towel for 15 minutes. On lightly floured surface, roll dough to thickness of about ¼ inch thick.

With a 2½-inch glass, cut as many circles as you can. Use the scraps of dough, kneading them again and cutting out more circles. Brush half of the circles lightly with the sesame-seed oil, and place an unoiled circle on top of an oiled one. Flatten each pair, with a rolling pin, to a diameter of about 6 inches. Turn it once to roll both sides, trying to keep its circular shape. Cover the pancakes with a dry towel.

Heat an 8-inch skillet (ungreased) to high heat. Reduce heat to moderate and cook the pancakes, one at a time, turning them over as little bubbles and brown specks appear. Cook about 1 minute on each side. As each pancake is cooked, gently separate the halves and stack them on a plate.

Makes approximately 24 pancakes.

chicken with mandarin oranges and almonds

2 ounces seedless raisins
1 jigger Madeira
1 large chicken, 3½ to 4 pounds, cut into serving pieces
2 teaspoons paprika
1 teaspoon white pepper
5 tablespoons oil
1 11-ounce can mandarin oranges, drained
1 clove garlic, minced
½ cup hot beef bouillon
1 tablespoon cornstarch
1 tablespoon soy sauce
½ teaspoon powdered ginger
½ cup heavy cream, lightly beaten
1 tablespoon butter
2 tablespoons sliced almonds

Cover raisins with Madeira and soak. Cut chicken into serving pieces. Mix together paprika and pepper, and rub chicken with this mixture. Heat oil in skillet or Dutch oven. Add chicken and fry until golden on all sides, about 10 minutes. Drain mandarin oranges, reserving juice. Measure ½ cup of juice and pour over chicken. Add minced garlic. Pour in beef bouillon, cover and simmer for 30 minutes. Drain raisins and add, cook for another 5 minutes.

Remove chicken with slotted spoon and arrange on preheated platter and keep warm. Blend cornstarch with small amount of cold water; add to sauce, stirring constantly until thickened and bubbly. Season with soy sauce and powdered ginger. Add mandarin oranges and lightly beaten heavy cream. Heat through, but do not boil. Heat butter in small skillet. Add sliced almonds and cook until golden. Pour sauce over chicken and top with almonds.

Makes 6 servings.

Picture on following pages:
chicken with mandarin oranges and almonds

chicken
with pineapple

chicken with pineapple

This is very good with rice.

1 chicken, approximately 2½ to 3 pounds, boned

marinade
2 tablespoons cornstarch
3 tablespoons oil
4 tablespoons soy sauce
1 tablespoon sherry
Salt
Pepper

2 tablespoons oil
1 cup pineapple chunks, drained, reserving pineapple juice

gravy
1 tablespoon oil
1 clove garlic, minced
½ cup pineapple juice
2 tablespoons sherry

Bone chicken and cut meat into bite-size pieces. Combine ingredients for marinade and blend thoroughly. Pour over chicken pieces, cover and refrigerate for 30 minutes. Heat 2 tablespoons oil in heavy skillet. Drain chicken, reserving marinade. Add chicken to skillet and brown for about 5 minutes while stirring constantly. Add drained pineapple chunks. Cover skillet and simmer over low heat for 12 minutes. Remove chicken and pineapple chunks with slotted spoon. Arrange on preheated platter and keep warm. Add additional 1 tablespoon oil to pan drippings. Stir in minced garlic and cook for 5 minutes. Blend pineapple juice with reserved marinade and sherry. Pour into skillet and heat through. Strain sauce through sieve, spoon over chicken and pineapple and serve immediately.

Makes 4 servings.

chicken cantonese

½ pound white meat of chicken sliced in strips, about 1½ inches
  long and ½ inch wide
½ pound snow peas, strings removed
¼ cup peanut oil
¼ cup bamboo shoots
1 cup bok choy, sliced
1 cup fresh mushrooms, sliced
1 cup celery, sliced diagonally
¼ cup water chestnuts, sliced
1 teaspoon MSG
4 cups chicken stock
2 tablespoons cornstarch mixed with ½ cup cold water

Slice chicken and set aside. Wash snow peas, remove strings and set
aside. Heat oil in skillet or wok and stir-fry chicken for about 10
seconds. Add bamboo shoots, bok choy, mushrooms, celery, water
chestnuts and MSG, and stir-fry for another 10 seconds. Add
chicken stock, bring to a boil, cover and simmer for about 1
minute. Stir in cornstarch mixture and mix thoroughly. Serve
immediately.

Makes 3 to 4 servings.

roast chicken chinese-style

4 scallions, chopped
2 small pieces fresh gingerroot
1 cup soy sauce
½ cup sherry
1 teaspoon sugar
¼ teaspoon salt
4 cups water
1 whole chicken, about 3 pounds
Scallions for garnish

Mix together chopped scallions, gingerroot, soy sauce, sherry,
sugar, and salt. Add water to stew pot. Mix in scallion mixture.
Bring to a boil. Wash chicken, place in pot, cover, and simmer for
30 minutes. Remove chicken from pot and place on roasting rack in
pan. Roast 45 minutes, or until chicken is tender and browned, in
350°F oven. Split chicken in half, and cut each half into 5 to 6
pieces. Arrange, skin-side-up, on serving platter. Garnish with
scallions. Serve the broth as a dipping sauce.

Makes 4 servings.

chinese
lemon chicken

1 3-pound chicken
1½ teaspoons salt, divided
2 tablespoons soy sauce
2 tablespoons brandy
5 tablespoons safflower oil
½ teaspoon powdered ginger
1 cup chicken broth
¼ cup lemon juice
½ teaspoon sugar

Rub inside of chicken with 1 teaspoon of the salt. Rub the outside with the soy sauce. Place in a deep bowl and pour the brandy over the chicken. Marinate for 6 hours, turning the chicken frequently. Drain and reserve marinade. In a wok over medium-high heat, combine the oil and ginger. Brown the chicken on all sides. Reduce the heat to low and add the marinade, chicken broth, lemon juice, sugar and remaining ½ teaspoon salt. Cover wok and simmer for about 25 minutes, or until the chicken is tender. Place on serving platter, cut into pieces, pour juices in wok over chicken and enjoy.

Makes 4 servings.

chicken balls
in oyster sauce

2 raw chicken breasts, skin and bones discarded
2 scallions
1 teaspoon salt
1 tablespoon cornstarch
1 tablespoon sherry
2 tablespoons water
Oil for frying
½ cup onions, thinly sliced
1 teaspoon sugar
½ teaspoon fresh gingerroot, chopped
2 tablespoons oyster sauce
¼ cup chicken broth
Freshly ground black pepper to taste

Chop the chicken and scallions together until very fine. Mix in the salt, cornstarch, sherry and water. Shape into small balls. Heat oil in skillet, and fry the balls until browned on all sides. Pour off the oil. Add the onions, sugar, ginger, oyster sauce and chicken broth. Cook and stir over low heat 5 minutes. Sprinkle with pepper.

Makes 4 servings.

chicken with rice

This is a quick, tasty dish—excellent for using up leftover chicken.

2 tablespoons oil
2 medium onions, diced
1 green pepper, diced
2 cups cooked rice
2 cups cooked chicken breast, diced
Soy sauce to taste
Dash of ginger

Heat oil in large skillet and brown onion. Add remaining ingredients and stir frequently while cooking over moderate heat 20 minutes.
Makes 2 servings.

sesame chicken

1 chicken, cut up, about 2½ to 3 pounds
Flour mixed with salt and pepper
2 eggs, beaten
2 tablespoons milk
1 cup flour mixed with ½ cup sesame seeds, ½ teaspoon salt and
   ¼ teaspoon pepper
Peanut oil for frying

cream sauce
4 tablespoons flour
4 tablespoons butter, melted
½ cup half-and-half
1 cup chicken stock
½ cup whipping cream
½ teaspoon salt or onion salt, if desired

Wash chicken and pat dry. Dust with flour mixed with salt and pepper. Mix beaten eggs with milk and dip chicken into this mixture. Then roll in the sesame-seed mixture. Fry in oil until light brown and tender.

To prepare the sauce, blend the flour into the butter over low heat, stirring constantly. Mix together the half-and-half, chicken stock and whipping cream. Gradually add to the butter and flour, stirring constantly. When smooth, stir in the salt or onion salt. Serve immediately with the chicken.
Makes 3 to 4 servings.

chinese duck

This recipe is worth the extra time it takes. This is excellent. My family enjoyed this duck very much.

2 cups sherry
½ cup honey
2 tablespoons soy sauce
2 tablespoons candied ginger, finely chopped
2 teaspoons powdered mustard
1 teaspoon sesame seeds
1 duck, 3 to 4 pounds
Salt
2 tablespoons margarine

orange sauce
6 oranges
1 piece of candied ginger, approximately size of a
  walnut, chopped
2 to 3 tablespoons sugar
¼ cup sherry
1 teaspoon cornstarch
1 11-ounce can mandarin orange sections
1 banana

garnish
1 orange, sliced
2 maraschino cherries
Parsley sprigs

Blend thoroughly sherry, honey, soy sauce, finely chopped ginger, mustard and sesame seeds. Pour over duck in large bowl, cover and refrigerate for 3 hours, turning duck occasionally. Remove duck and drain well on paper toweling. Reserve marinade. Salt inside of duck lightly. Heat margarine in large skillet or Dutch oven. Add duck and brown well on all sides. Place duck in preheated 350°F oven and cook for 1 hour and 10 minutes, basting occasionally with reserved marinade.

To prepare sauce, pare half an orange and cut rind into thin strips. Now squeeze oranges. Blend orange juice, sliced rind and chopped ginger. Add sugar and half the sherry. Heat mixture in saucepan. Blend rest of sherry with cornstarch, and slowly add to Orange Sauce, stirring constantly until thick and bubbly. Drain mandarin orange sections and slice banana. Add half of the fruit to sauce. Place duck on preheated platter. Garnish with rest of mandarins, banana and orange slices, cherries and parsley. Serve sauce separately.

Makes approximately 4 servings.

Picture on following pages: chinese duck

chicken chow mein

chicken chow mein

1 green sweet pepper, cut
   into slices
1 red sweet pepper, cut
   into slices
1 cup boiling water
1½ tablespoons butter
1 small onion, chopped
2 stalks celery, sliced
1 tablespoon flour
1 cup chicken broth
2 tablespoons soy sauce
Freshly ground pepper to taste

1 4-ounce can sliced
   mushrooms, drained
8 ounces cooked chicken
   breast, cut into
   bite-size pieces
6 cups water
8 ounces egg noodles
Salt
1 tablespoon butter
Oil for frying
4 ounces sliced almonds,
   toasted and slightly salted

Cut green and red peppers into slices. Blanch in boiling water for 5 minutes. Remove and drain. Heat 1½ tablespoons butter in saucepan. Add onions and celery and sauté until onions are transparent. Sprinkle with flour, pour in chicken broth and bring to a boil while stirring constantly. Simmer for 10 minutes. Season with soy sauce and pepper. Add pepper slices, drained mushrooms, and chicken pieces. Cover and simmer for 15 minutes.

Meanwhile, bring 6 cups of slightly salted water to a boil and add noodles and cook for 15 minutes. Drain and rinse with cold water. Set aside ⅓ of the noodles. Place rest of noodles in heated bowl, add 1 tablespoon butter, cover and keep warm.

Heat oil in skillet until very hot. Cut noodles that were set aside into approximately 2-inch-long pieces. Add to hot oil and fry until golden. Drain on paper towels. To serve, spoon chicken mixture over buttered noodles; top with fried noodles and toasted almonds.
Makes 4 servings.

seafood

shrimp with mandarin oranges

2 teaspoons sherry
1 teaspoon cornstarch
½ pound shrimp, cleaned
Oil for cooking
½ cup drained canned mandarin orange segments
¼ teaspoon sugar
¼ teaspoon salt

Mix together sherry and cornstarch and marinate shrimp in mixture for 5 minutes. Heat oil in skillet or wok, enough to cover bottom of pan, and stir-fry shrimp just until color changes. Add mandarin orange segments, sugar, and salt and stir-fry just until heated through, no more than 1 minute.

Makes 2 servings.

shrimp with cucumber

1 pound uncooked shrimp
1 tablespoon sherry
2 teaspoons salt, divided
1 teaspoon sugar
2 teaspoons cornstarch
2 cucumbers, peeled and cut into 1-inch pieces with
   seeds removed
Oil for sautéing

Shell and devein the shrimp. Wash and drain. Cut in half lengthwise and then cut each half into 2 pieces crosswise. Combine shrimp with sherry, 1 teaspoon salt, sugar and cornstarch. Prepare the cucumbers and set aside. Heat oil in saucepan over high heat and sauté the cucumber. Add the rest of the salt and stir until cucumber is slightly transparent, about 4 minutes. In another saucepan heat oil over high heat and sauté the shrimp until they turn pink. Add cucumber, mix well and cook for another 2 minutes.

Makes 2 to 3 servings.

shrimp and bean sprouts

1 cup celery, sliced diagonally
1 cup fresh mushrooms, sliced
½ cup scallions, sliced
Oil for cooking
½ pound fresh bean sprouts
½ pound cooked shrimp
Soy sauce to taste

Prepare celery, mushrooms and scallions. Heat oil in skillet or wok and stir-fry celery until it turns bright green. Add mushrooms and scallions and stir-fry for 1 minute. Add bean sprouts and shrimp and toss lightly until heated through, approximately 2 minutes. Sprinkle with soy sauce and enjoy.

Makes 2 servings.

hot-mustard shrimp

3 tablespoons powdered mustard
¼ teaspoon salt
1 teaspoon sugar
1 teaspoon horseradish
¾ cup flat beer
1 pound shrimp, cleaned
4 tablespoons melted butter
Duck sauce

Mix mustard, salt, sugar and horseradish together. Add enough beer to make a smooth paste. Gradually add rest of beer to make it thin. Let mixture stand for 1 hour. If it becomes too thick, add more beer or cold water.

Dip shrimp in mustard sauce, skewer and brush with melted butter. Grill on hibachi or grill for approximately 8 minutes. Turn frequently for even browning. Serve with duck sauce.

Makes 2 to 3 servings.

shrimp and asparagus

1 pound cooked shrimp, shelled and deveined
1 can water chestnuts, drained and sliced
1 medium onion, sliced
1 cup fresh mushrooms, sliced
1 cup celery, sliced diagonally
1 small can mandarin oranges, drained
1½ pounds fresh asparagus, steamed
2 tablespoons oil
¼ teaspoon salt
½ teaspoon freshly ground black pepper
2 tablespoons sugar
2 tablespoons soy sauce
Cooked rice

Prepare the shrimp and set aside. Drain and slice the water chestnuts. On a large tray arrange the shrimp, chestnuts, onion, mushrooms, celery, mandarin oranges, and asparagus. Heat the oil in a wok. Add onion, celery, salt, pepper, and sugar. Stir-fry until the vegetables are tender, but still on the crisp side. Add asparagus and shrimp. Place the water chestnuts and mushrooms over the shrimp. Sprinkle with the soy sauce and place the orange sections on top. Cover and cook until mixture steams. Reduce heat and simmer about 10 minutes. Serve with rice.

Makes 6 servings.

sesame shrimp

½ cup sesame seeds, toasted
1 pound shrimp, cleaned
Salt
Freshly ground black pepper
6 tablespoons melted butter

Place sesame seeds in ungreased skillet over low heat and stir until browned. Set aside. Sprinkle shrimp lightly with salt and pepper. Dip in melted butter. Roll in toasted sesame seeds. Skewer shrimp and grill approximately 8 minutes over a grill or hibachi, turning frequently to brown evenly.

Makes 2 to 3 servings.

grilled oriental shrimp

1 pound shrimp, cleaned
⅓ cup soy sauce
¼ cup sesame oil
1 tablespoon brown sugar
1 tablespoon finely chopped fresh gingerroot or ¾ teaspoon
   powdered ginger
3 scallions, finely chopped

Combine all ingredients and marinate in refrigerator 6 hours. Drain the shrimp, reserving the marinade. Skewer the shrimp and grill over a grill or hibachi approximately 5 minutes, turning frequently and basting with marinade.

Makes 2 to 3 servings.

crab rangoon

¼ pound crab meat, chopped
¼ pound cream cheese
¼ teaspoon A-1 sauce
⅛ teaspoon garlic powder
Won ton squares
1 egg yolk, beaten
Oil for deep frying

Blend chopped crab meat with cream cheese, A-1 sauce, and garlic powder. Put ½ teaspoon of mixture in center of each won ton square. Fold square over cornerwise, moisten edges with beaten egg yolk and twist together. Fry in oil until lightly browned. Drain, and serve hot.

Makes approximately 95 filled won ton squares.

oriental-style tuna casserole

1 small can tuna
½ cup diced onion
½ cup diced celery
2 cups fresh bean sprouts or 1 can bean sprouts
¼ cup diced green pepper
Soy sauce to taste

Drain tuna and mix with onion, celery, bean sprouts, green pepper, and soy sauce to taste. If fresh bean sprouts are used, blanch in colander and rinse with cold water. Drain well. If canned bean sprouts are used, drain, rinse with cold water and drain well. Place in casserole and bake at 350°F for 30 minutes. Add additional soy sauce, if desired.

Makes 2 to 3 servings.

fish roll

3 eggs, beaten
1 tablespoon water
2 tablespoons oil
¾ cup chopped flounder
2 tablespoons water chestnuts, chopped
2 tablespoons scallions, chopped
Salt to taste
1 tablespoon soy sauce
Flour

sauce
1½ tablespoons soy sauce
1 tablespoon cornstarch
¾ cup water
½ teaspoon sugar

Beat the eggs with the water. Heat a little of the oil in a large skillet and fry half of the egg mixture until it's set. Turn it over and cook the other side. Repeat this with the rest of the egg mixture. Mix together the fish, water chestnuts, scallions, salt and soy sauce. Put half of it on one of the egg pieces, covering the whole thing. Roll it up jelly-roll style, put some flour on the edges and press together. Repeat with the other piece of egg. With a sharp knife, cut the rolls into ¼-inch slices. Heat oil in skillet and fry the slices until golden brown.

To make the sauce, mix together the soy sauce and cornstarch until smooth. Blend in water and sugar and place in small saucepan. Boil slowly for about 3 minutes. Serve the sauce separately.

Makes 5 to 6 servings.

fish tempura

2 pounds fresh fish fillets
Salt to taste
Lemon juice
½ recipe Basic Tempura Batter
Oil
Chili–Horseradish Sauce
Soy sauce

basic tempura batter
2 cups all-purpose flour, sifted
3 egg yolks
2 cups ice water

Cut the fish fillets into bite-size pieces and drain well on paper toweling. Prepare other ingredients. Season the fish with salt and squeeze desired amount of lemon juice over fish. Make up the batter.

Sift flour 3 times. Combine the yolks and water in a large bowl over ice and beat with a whisk until well-blended. Gradually add the flour, stirring and turning the mixture with a spoon. Don't overmix. Keep the batter over ice while frying. Makes approximately 4½ cups.

Place all the fish in the batter. When ready to fry, remove the fish from the batter with a fork and drain slightly. Heat the oil in a wok, an electric skillet or deep-fat fryer to between 350 and 375°F. Fry the fish, a few pieces at a time, for about 5 minutes, turning to brown evenly. Remove the fish from the oil with a slotted spoon and drain well on paper toweling. Keep fish warm until all is cooked. Serve with Chili–Horseradish Sauce (recipe follows) or just dipped into soy sauce. Use this batter for vegetables also, or meat, or seafood. Skim off loose particles of food as they appear, to keep the oil clean. Keep the batter cold.

chili–horseradish sauce
1 cup mayonnaise
⅓ cup chili sauce
3 tablespoons horseradish

Combine all ingredients in small bowl and mix thoroughly. Chill well before serving.
Makes approximately 1½ cups.

fish tempura

chinese fish

1 whole trout, about 1 pound
1 whole carp, about 3 pounds
Juice of 1 lemon
Salt
White pepper
2 slices lean bacon
Margarine to grease pan
4 large leaves savoy cabbage (if unavailable, use regular cabbage)
1 pound fresh mushrooms
2 pieces sugared ginger
3 tablespoons soy sauce
Pinch of ground anise
1 cup hot water
2 teaspoons cornstarch
2 tablespoons bacon drippings
Juice of half a lemon

garnish
2 tablespoons chopped parsley
Lemon slices

Have fishmonger scale and clean out the insides of the fish, but leave whole. At home wash fish thoroughly under running water, pat dry and rub with lemon juice. With sharp knife make shallow incisions in backs of both fish and rub with salt and pepper. Cut bacon into small strips and insert one strip in each incision. Grease ovenproof baking dish with margarine and line with cabbage leaves. Place fish on top. Slice mushrooms and sugared ginger. Mix together and spoon over fish.

Sprinkle with soy sauce and ground anise. Pour in small amount of hot water. Cover with lid or aluminum foil and place in preheated oven at 350°F. Bake for 30 minutes. While baking, gradually add rest of hot water and baste fish with pan drippings.

Remove fish and cabbage leaves from pan. Arrange on a preheated platter. Bring pan drippings to a boil, scraping all brown particles from bottom of pan and adding some more water, if necessary. Blend cornstarch with small amount of cold water, add to pan drippings and stir until sauce is smooth and bubbly. Correct seasoning if necessary, and serve separately. Melt and heat bacon drippings. Pour over fish and sprinkle with lemon juice. Garnish fish with chopped parsley and lemon slices.

Makes approximately 4 servings.

chinese fish

steamed
whole fish

1½ pounds whole fish (flounder, pike, trout, or sea bass)
1 teaspoon salt
½ teaspoon freshly ground pepper
¼ teaspoon powdered ginger
3 cups water
2 teaspoons mixed pickling spices (or more if you prefer it spicier)
2 bay leaves
2 cloves garlic, cut in half
2 tablespoons chopped scallion

garnish
Lemon slices
Tomato
Parsley

Have fish scaled and cleaned and head removed, if you prefer. Lightly score the skin so seasonings will flavor the fish. Combine salt, pepper, and ginger and rub on fish thoroughly. Pour water into large frying pan or wok and add pickling spices, bay leaves, garlic, and scallion. Place rack in pan or wok so that the fish will sit above the liquid, in order to allow the steam to circulate. Place the fish on the rack, cover and let simmer for approximately 30 minutes, or until fish is tender. Garnish with lemon slices, tomato, and parsley.

Makes 3 servings.

halibut
cantonese

1½ pounds halibut, cut into small chunks
1 tablespoon oil
1 medium onion, chopped

sauce
1½ cups water
1 tablespoon oil
Pinch salt
3 teaspoons soy sauce
1 teaspoon MSG
Pinch of freshly ground pepper
2 tablespoons cornstarch dissolved in 3 tablespoons water

2 cloves garlic, minced
1 scallion, sliced
1 tablespoon celery, chopped
1 egg, beaten

Boil the halibut in a pot of water for 2 minutes. Heat the oil in a skillet and brown the onions. Transfer the fish to the skillet. Mix together the sauce ingredients, except for the cornstarch and water. Pour the sauce on the fish, and add the garlic, scallion and celery. Cover the skillet and simmer for 2 minutes. Pour the beaten egg slowly into the sauce, mixing constantly. Mix cornstarch with water and stir into sauce. Cook until thickened.

Makes 2 servings.

vegetables

chinese fried vegetables

Oil for cooking
½ cup celery, sliced diagonally
4 ounces bamboo shoots
4 ounces water chestnuts, sliced
3 scallions, sliced into 1-inch pieces
½ cup fresh mushrooms
1 cup bean sprouts, fresh or canned
Soy sauce to taste

Heat oil in skillet or wok. Add celery, bamboo shoots and water chestnuts. Stir-fry for 2 minutes. Add scallions, mushrooms and bean sprouts and stir-fry for 1 minute or until heated through. Sprinkle with soy sauce to taste and serve immediately.

Makes 2 servings.

ethel's grow-your-own bean sprouts

There is nothing like growing your own bean sprouts to have them available when you desire and to know that they are fresh. It's a very simple procedure and takes very little time. All you need is a package of mung beans (bean sprouts), a quart jar, water, and a strainer.

Soak ¼ cup mung beans in a quart jar overnight. Pour off the water, use a strainer if desired, and place the jar in a dark place for 3 days, rinsing the beans 3 times a day and draining them thoroughly after each rinsing. At the end of 3 days you will have ready-to-eat, home-grown bean sprouts. Refrigerate and use as needed.

stir-fried celery and bean sprouts

2 cups celery, sliced diagonally
Oil
4 cups fresh bean sprouts
Sprinkles of soy sauce

Slice celery and set aside. Heat oil in skillet and stir-fry celery for about 2 minutes, until bright green and tender but still crisp. Add bean sprouts and stir-fry for 1 minute, or until bean sprouts are heated through. Sprinkle with soy sauce to taste and serve immediately.

Makes 2 servings.

pea-pod casserole

1 package frozen pea pods, boiled
1 can water chestnuts, sliced
2 cups fresh bean sprouts, or 1 can bean sprouts
1 can cream of mushroom soup
1 can onion rings (optional)

Boil pea pods for 2 minutes. Drain and place in casserole dish. Place sliced water chestnuts on top of pea pods. Next, place a layer of bean sprouts. If fresh sprouts are used, first blanch, then rinse with cold water and drain well. If canned bean sprouts are used, drain, rinse with cold water and drain well. Cover with cream of mushroom soup. Bake for 15 minutes at 350°F. Place onion rings on top and heat again for about 2 or 3 minutes.

Makes 4 servings.

grilled green peppers

2 green peppers, cut into 1-inch squares
Melted butter or meat marinade

Parboil peppers gently for 2 minutes. Drain and dry. Brush with melted butter or marinade. Skewer and cook on a hibachi or grill for 4 minutes.

Makes 2 servings.

ellen's marinated bean sprouts

This is a delicious salad with a very unique flavor. It's a favorite of ours!

1 pound fresh bean sprouts
3 tablespoons chopped scallions (use green and white parts)
2 tablespoons sesame-seed oil
2 tablespoons soy sauce
1 tablespoon vodka
1 tablespoon vinegar

Place bean sprouts in colander and blanch. Immediately rinse with cold water and drain well. In large bowl combine remaining ingredients and place bean sprouts in mixture to marinate at room temperature for 1 hour. Refrigerate for at least 3 hours before serving.

Makes 4 servings.

frying-pan bean sprouts

This is an excellent recipe to make in a wok.

2 cups fresh bean sprouts
Oil for frying—enough to cover bottom of pan
Sprinkles of soy sauce
Chopped scallion (optional)

Place bean sprouts in colander and rinse well with cold water. Drain well. Heat oil in frying pan until hot. Place bean sprouts in pan and toss until heated through. Cook quickly on high heat. Remove to serving plate and sprinkle with soy sauce to taste. If desired, chopped scallion may be added when cooking.

Makes 2 servings.

bean sprouts with celery and mushrooms

2 tablespoons oil
3 stalks celery, sliced diagonally
1 onion, chopped
¼ pound fresh mushrooms, sliced
½ cup chicken stock
1 tablespoon soy sauce
½ teaspoon MSG
1 pound fresh bean sprouts
1 tablespoon cornstarch mixed with ¼ cup cold water

Add oil to preheated pan. Sauté celery, onion, and mushrooms until onion is soft. Add chicken stock, soy sauce, and MSG. Bring to a boil and add bean sprouts. Stir-fry only for about 30 seconds. Cover and simmer 3 seconds. Thicken with cornstarch mixture, adding it a little at a time. Serve immediately.

Makes 4 servings.

64

delicious chinese cabbage

1 Chinese cabbage
½ cup water
1 tablespoon salt
1 tablespoon sesame oil
½ cup shredded carrot
2 tablespoons shredded gingerroot
1 tablespoon sugar
½ teaspoon salt
2 tablespoons vinegar
Few drops Tabasco

Slice cabbage, sprinkle with water and salt and let stand overnight. Squeeze water from cabbage and arrange on serving platter. Heat oil in skillet or wok to medium-high heat and sauté carrot and ginger for approximately 3 minutes. Add sugar, salt, vinegar and a few drops of Tabasco. Bring to a boil. Pour over cabbage. Let stand at least 15 minutes before serving.

Makes 4 servings.

cabbage and mushrooms

1 pound cabbage
2 tablespoons oil
2 cloves garlic, crushed
½ cup fresh mushrooms, sliced
½ teaspoon sugar
½ teaspoon soy sauce

Cut cabbage into bite-size pieces and set aside. Heat oil in skillet to medium-high heat and sauté garlic approximately 3 minutes. Discard garlic. Add cabbage and sauté for 2 minutes. Add mushrooms, sugar and soy sauce and mix well to heat through. Serve immediately.

Makes 4 servings.

chinese mushrooms in chicken broth

1½ cups dried mushrooms, sliced
2 cups chicken broth
1 scallion
1 ½-inch slice of fresh gingerroot
¼ cup soy sauce
1 teaspoon sugar
1 teaspoon salt
1 tablespoon cornstarch blended with small amount
  chicken broth
Cooked rice

Soak the mushrooms in the chicken broth for 30 minutes. Place broth and mushrooms in wok. Add scallion and ginger. Bring to boil. Cover and reduce heat. Simmer for 1 hour. Remove scallion and ginger. Stir in soy sauce, sugar and salt. Blend cornstarch with small amount of broth and stir into mixture in wok slowly. Cook, stirring constantly, until slightly thickened. Serve this over cooked rice.

Makes approximately 2 cups.

65

delicious spinach

1 pound fresh spinach, washed and cut into 2-inch pieces
2 tablespoons oil
Salt to taste
1 small can bamboo shoots
8 fresh mushrooms, sliced
¼ cup chicken broth

Wash and cut the spinach into pieces. Heat oil in wok or skillet. Add salt and spinach and stir-fry for 2 minutes. Add bamboo shoots, mushrooms, and chicken broth. Mix, cover and simmer for about 2 minutes, or until heated through.

Makes 2 servings.

cooked spinach

½ pound spinach
1 tablespoon oil
1 clove garlic, crushed
½ cup chicken stock, warmed
Salt to taste
Sugar to taste
1 teaspoon soy sauce
½ teaspoon cornstarch
2 teaspoons water

Wash spinach and tear into bite-size pieces. Drain well and set aside. Heat oil in skillet or wok and fry garlic until lightly browned. Discard garlic. Add spinach and stir-fry for 1 minute. Add chicken stock, salt, sugar, and soy sauce. Simmer for 2 minutes. Mix together cornstarch and water and slowly stir into spinach mixture. Simmer for 1 minute. Serve immediately.

Makes 2 servings.

fresh-spinach salad

10 ounces fresh spinach
4 ounces fresh mushrooms
¼ cup chopped scallion
Small amount soy sauce
Sesame seeds (optional)

Thoroughly wash spinach and tear up larger pieces. Drain well. Slice mushrooms and add to spinach. Add chopped scallion and toss well. Sprinkle with the amount of soy sauce desired and toss lightly. Sprinkle each portion with sesame seeds.

Makes 4 servings.

baked chinese cabbage

baked chinese cabbage

2 heads Chinese cabbage
4 cups beef bouillon
1 small onion, coarsely chopped
Margarine to grease ovenproof baking dish
6 tablespoons grated cheese, Emmenthal or Gruyère
2 tablespoons butter or margarine

sauce
½ cup sour cream
2 tablespoons chopped parsley
1 small onion, chopped
Salt to taste
White pepper to taste
1½ tablespoons grated cheese, Emmenthal or Gruyère

Remove outer wilted leaves from cabbage and cut cabbage in half lengthwise. Cut each half into 3 or 4 pieces. Wash thoroughly and pat dry. Bring beef bouillon to boil, add onion and cabbage and simmer for 20 minutes. Remove cabbage with slotted spoon and drain. Grease ovenproof baking dish with margarine. Place ⅓ of cabbage in dish, sprinkle with ⅓ of cheese, and dot with ⅓ of butter or margarine. Repeat this until cabbage, cheese, and butter are used.

Prepare sauce by combining and stirring thoroughly sour cream, parsley, onion, salt, and pepper. Pour over cabbage. Sprinkle with 1½ tablespoons grated cheese. Bake in preheated 375°F oven until cheese melts completely, approximately 10 to 15 minutes.

Makes approximately 4 servings.

mixed chinese vegetables

mixed chinese vegetables

5 large dried Chinese mushrooms
1 cup lukewarm water
5 ounces green cabbage
4 ounces carrots
4 ounces cucumber
5 ounces canned bamboo shoots
4 tablespoons sesame-seed oil
2 ounces frozen peas
½ cup hot chicken broth
2 tablespoons soy sauce
Salt
Pinch of sugar
Pinch of MSG

Soak mushrooms in water for 30 minutes. Shred cabbage, cut carrots, cucumber and bamboo shoots into julienne strips. Cube mushrooms. Heat oil in skillet, add cabbage and cook for 2 minutes. Add mushrooms, cucumbers, carrots and bamboo shoots and peas. Pour in chicken broth. Season with soy sauce, salt, sugar and MSG. Simmer over low heat for 15 minutes. Serve immediately.

Makes 2 servings.

fruited rice salads

fruited rice salads

2 tablespoons butter
½ cup celery, diced
¼ cup onion, minced
2 teaspoons grated orange rind
1 cup orange juice
1 cup water
½ teaspoon poultry seasoning
1 cup long-grain rice
⅓ cup golden raisins
6 orange shells

Heat the butter in medium-sized saucepan and sauté the celery and onion until tender. Stir in the orange rind, juice, water, poultry seasoning, rice and raisins. Bring to a boil. Stir well, reduce heat and cover. Simmer until liquid is absorbed and rice is tender, about 30 minutes. Remove from heat. When cool, refrigerate for several hours. Serve in orange shells.

Makes 6 servings.

cucumber salad

2 large cucumbers
⅓ cup white rice vinegar or white vinegar diluted with a little water
3½ teaspoons sugar
¾ teaspoon salt
2 slices fresh gingerroot, finely chopped

Cut cucumbers in half lengthwise and remove seeds; peel and slice crosswise into very thin slices. Mix together vinegar, sugar, salt, and ginger. Place sliced cucumbers in marinade and refrigerate for at least 2 hours before serving.

Makes 4 to 6 servings.

fried rice

fried rice

½ pound long-grain rice
½ pound cooked ham, cut into strips
1 6-ounce can shrimp, drained
3 tablespoons oil
2 tablespoons soy sauce
1 leek, sliced
4 eggs
Freshly ground black pepper

Cook rice according to package directions. Cut ham into strips. Drain shrimp. Heat oil in large skillet, add ham and shrimp and cook until lightly browned, approximately 5 minutes. Add rice and soy sauce. Cook another 5 minutes. Add leek and cook for an additional 5 minutes, stirring occasionally. Lightly beat eggs with pepper. Pour over rice and cook until eggs are set. Serve on preheated platter.

Makes 4 servings.

gail's fried rice

This is an excellent recipe for using leftover rice. Use the amount of mushrooms and scallions suitable for whatever amount of rice you have. You may also add leftover chicken. Experiment putting in different ingredients and different amounts of ingredients until you discover how your family likes it best. If you like fried rice, you'll love this!

Oil, salad or peanut
Rice, cooked and chilled
Mushrooms, fresh or canned
Scallions, chopped
Soy sauce
Beaten egg

Heat oil in skillet. Add rice, mushrooms, drained, if canned, or sliced if fresh, scallions and soy sauce. Cook over low heat about 10 to 15 minutes, stirring occasionally. Add beaten egg; cook and stir another 2 to 3 minutes. Serve with additional soy sauce.

fried rice

2 tablespoons oil
1 green pepper, chopped
½ cup fresh mushrooms, sliced
3 cups cooked cold rice
½ cup cooked chicken or beef (leftover)
Soy sauce to taste

Heat oil in skillet to medium-high heat. Sauté pepper and mushrooms until pepper just begins to get soft. Add rice and chicken or beef and sauté until hot, approximately 5 minutes, stirring frequently. Sprinkle with soy sauce to taste.

Makes 4 servings.

chinese rice

1 cup medium or long-grain rice
Cold water

Put rice in heavy pan that has a tight-fitting lid. Add cold water until it is about 1 inch above the rice. Place pan over high heat and boil, uncovered, until most of the water has been absorbed, stirring often to prevent sticking. Turn heat to lowest setting, place lid on pan, and let rice steam for approximately 20 minutes, depending upon how soft you like rice. (Do not lift the lid while rice is steaming.)

Makes approximately 4 servings.

cole slaw with sesame dressing

This is an unusual and tasty salad to go along with your Chinese meal.

3 cups shredded cabbage
2 medium carrots, shredded
½ medium onion, grated

sesame dressing
¼ cup sesame seeds, toasted
1½ tablespoons lemon juice
1½ tablespoons vinegar
1 teaspoon sugar
1 tablespoon soy sauce
¼ teaspoon MSG
¼ cup peanut oil

Combine cabbage, carrots, and onion.

Place sesame seeds in ungreased skillet over low heat and stir until lightly browned. Grind toasted seeds in blender. Add lemon juice, vinegar, sugar, soy sauce, and MSG, and blend into smooth paste. Combine mixture with peanut oil and blend well. Mix thoroughly with cabbage mixture and enjoy!

Makes 4 servings.

zucchini chinese-style

2 pounds zucchini, sliced in ¼-inch slices
½ pound fresh mushrooms, sliced
¼ cup oil
1 tablespoon soy sauce
½ cup chicken broth
2 teaspoons cornstarch mixed with 4 teaspoons cold water

Wash and slice zucchini, and set aside. Wash and slice mushrooms. Heat oil in skillet and sauté mushrooms for a few seconds. Add zucchini and stir-fry until zucchini is coated with oil. Add soy sauce and chicken broth. Bring to a boil, cover and simmer until zucchini is bright green and just tender and still crisp. Thicken with cornstarch mixture and serve immediately.

Makes approximately 6 servings.

string beans chinese-style

2 cloves garlic, minced
1 medium onion, chopped
1 tablespoon oil
2 tablespoons soy sauce
1 pound fresh string beans
1 cup chicken broth

Mince garlic, chop onion and set aside. Heat oil in skillet to medium-high. Sauté garlic and onion until golden. Add soy sauce and string beans. Pour in the chicken broth, turn temperature down and let mixture simmer for approximately 7 to 8 minutes, until beans are tender, but still crisp.

Makes 4 servings.

pickled pineapple

2 pineapples, peeled and sliced in 1-inch rings
2 tablespoons cloves
2 cups water
4 cups sugar
2½ cups white vinegar
2 sticks cinnamon

Peel and slice pineapple, then core and cut into 1-inch pieces. Tie cloves in small piece of cheesecloth. In large saucepan combine water, sugar, vinegar, cinnamon and cloves. Bring to a boil and cook over low heat 20 minutes. Add the pineapple, cover and cook over low heat 15 to 20 minutes, or until pineapple is tender and clear. Pack in sterile jars.

Makes approximately 3 to 4 pints.

sweet-potato balls

1½ pounds sweet potatoes
½ cup flour
5 tablespoons sugar
¼ teaspoon salt
1 beaten egg
Oil for deep-frying
Powdered sugar

Peel sweet potatoes and boil until very soft. Mash and remove any stringy fibers. Mix with flour, sugar, salt and egg and form small balls. Deep-fry in oil over medium heat until lightly browned. Drain on paper toweling and sprinkle with powdered sugar.

Makes 2½ dozen balls.

sweet-potato and banana casserole

This is very tasty.

4 medium sweet potatoes
4 tablespoons butter
1½ teaspoons salt
4 bananas, sliced
¾ cup brown sugar
¾ cup orange juice

Cook the sweet potatoes in boiling water until tender but still firm. Cool. Peel and slice ¼ inch thick. Place in buttered casserole in alternate layers, dotted with butter and sprinkled with salt, with bananas sprinkled with brown sugar. End the top layer with bananas, dotted with butter. Add orange juice. Bake in a 350°F oven for about 30 minutes, or until the top is browned.

Makes 6 servings.

73

egg noodles with mushrooms

This is a nice change from rice.

8 ounces fine egg noodles
2 tablespoons oil
1 cup bamboo shoots
1 cup sliced almonds

1 cup fresh mushrooms, sliced
½ cup chicken broth
3 tablespoons soy sauce
Salt to taste

Cook noodles according to package directions for 8 minutes. Drain. Heat oil in a wok. Stir-fry noodles for 3 minutes. Stir in the bamboo shoots, almonds, and mushrooms, and mix thoroughly. Stir in the broth, soy sauce, and salt. Simmer, covered, until the liquid is almost gone.

Makes approximately 8 servings.

cauliflower chinese-style

1 small cauliflower
2 tablespoons oil
¼ pound fresh mushrooms, sliced
1 cup chicken broth, warmed
2 tablespoons soy sauce
½ teaspoon MSG
1 tablespoon cornstarch mixed with ¼ cup cold water

Trim cauliflower, wash, and separate into florets. Slice large florets. Pour oil into preheated pan. Add cauliflower and sauté lightly. Add mushrooms and sauté a few seconds longer. Add chicken broth, soy sauce and MSG. Bring to a boil, cover and simmer until cauliflower is done, but still crisp. Thicken with cornstarch mixture, adding it slowly.

Makes approximately 4 servings.

chinese cauliflower with noodles

This is an unusual and tasty dish.

1 small head of cauliflower
2 tablespoons oil, divided
½ pound thinly sliced beef
Salt to taste
1 small onion, chopped
2 tablespoons soy sauce
1 cup beef bouillon
1 teaspoon cornstarch
½ teaspoon cold water
½ pound egg noodles

Clean cauliflower and divide into small florets. Heat 1 tablespoon oil in heavy skillet. Add cauliflower and beef slices and cook until lightly browned. Season with salt. Add chopped onion and soy sauce and cook for 5 minutes. Pour in beef bouillon and simmer for 35 minutes. Blend cornstarch with cold water. Stir into cauliflower mixture until slightly thick and bubbly.

Cook egg noodles in 3 quarts of salted water for 10 minutes. Drain. Heat other tablespoon of oil in skillet, add noodles and fry until golden. Mix noodles with cauliflower. Heat through and serve.

Makes 4 servings.

sweet-and-sour yams and pineapple

sweet-and-sour yams and pineapple

1 20-ounce can sliced pineapple; drain and reserve syrup
1 tablespoon cornstarch
¼ teaspoon salt
3 tablespoons fresh lemon juice
2 1-pound cans of yams, drained
Oil
4 scallions, sliced
1 small green pepper, cut into small chunks
½ cup celery, sliced diagonally

Drain pineapple; reserve syrup. In saucepan, combine reserved syrup, cornstarch and salt. Blend well. Bring to a boil over medium heat. Cook until thickened, stirring constantly. Stir in the lemon juice. Arrange pineapple and yams in casserole and pour the sauce over mixture. Bake, covered, in a 350°F oven for about 30 minutes or until hot. In small amount of oil in skillet, sauté scallions, green pepper chunks and celery until just tender, but still crisp. Stir carefully into yam mixture. Serve immediately.
Makes approximately 8 servings.

chinese cauliflower with noodles

desserts

almond cookies

1 cup shortening
1 cup sugar
1 egg, beaten
3 cups sifted flour

1½ teaspoons baking soda
3 tablespoons almond extract
4 tablespoons honey or corn syrup
1 cup blanched almonds

Cream together shortening and sugar. Add egg. Slowly add flour, baking soda, almond extract and honey and blend until smooth. Take a small piece of dough and roll it into a ball. Repeat until all dough is used. Flatten each ball to about ½ inch thickness. Place an almond in the center of each. Bake on greased cookie sheet in preheated 375°F oven for about 15 to 20 minutes.

In China lard is the usual ingredient in Almond Cookies, but you may substitute margarine.

Makes approximately 4 dozen cookies.

simple rice dessert

This is, as the name implies, a very simple and yummy dessert. Experiment with different fruits, or different proportions.

1 cup leftover cooked rice
1 cup canned drained fruit, such as pineapple, peaches, mandarin oranges, fruit cocktail
2 cups whipped cream

Mix rice with drained fruit (cut into slices if necessary) and fold in whipped cream. Serve in dessert dishes.

Makes approximately 4 servings.

chinese honey shortbread

chinese honey shortbread

These are delicious with tea!

2½ cups all purpose flour
Pinch of salt
½ cup butter
½ cup honey

In a medium-sized bowl, place flour and salt. Mix the butter into the flour with the fingers until mixture is like fine meal. Add the honey gradually and, still working with the fingers, blend until dough is smooth and leaves the side of the bowl. From a piece of cardboard, cut a fan-shaped pattern. Roll out the dough on lightly floured surface to about ¼ inch thick and cut into fan shapes. Place on baking sheet that has been lightly floured and cut 6 deep slashes lengthwise as shown in picture. Bake in preheated 350°F oven until lightly browned, about 12 minutes.
Makes approximately 2½ dozen "fans."

delicious fruit dressing

This is a scrumptious sauce, delicious poured over any kind of fruit.

1 cup sugar
1 egg, well beaten

Juice and grated rind of 1 orange,
1 lime, and 1 lemon

Combine all ingredients in saucepan and blend well. Cook over medium heat, stirring constantly, until mixture comes to a boil. Boil 1 minute. Remove from heat, cool, and store in refrigerator in covered jar. Serve as an accompaniment to a dessert of fresh fruit.
Makes approximately 1 pint of dressing.

spiced mandarin oranges

spiced mandarin oranges

1 small tangerine (an orange may be substituted)
2 11-ounce cans mandarin oranges
¼ cup water
⅓ cup firmly packed brown sugar
1 2-inch piece of stick cinnamon

Cut the peeling from the tangerine in paper-thin strips. Squeeze the juice and strain. In medium-sized saucepan, combine the peeling and juice with the rest of the ingredients. Simmer for 15 minutes. Remove from heat and remove the peeling and cinnamon. Chill for several hours. Serve in small dessert dishes.

Makes approximately 4 servings.

sesame cookies

1 cup sifted cake flour
½ stick butter
½ cup sugar
¼ teaspoon salt

1 egg
1 egg yolk mixed with
   1 tablespoon water
Sesame seeds

Combine flour, butter, sugar, salt and egg in bowl and knead well until it forms a soft dough. Place on well-floured board and form into long roll about 1½ inches in diameter. Cut into approximately 36 pieces and flatten each with bottom of glass dipped in flour. Brush one side of cookie with egg-yolk and water mixture. Sprinkle sesame seeds on brushed side and press sesame seeds to cookie. Place on greased cookie sheet and bake at 350°F for 10 to 12 minutes.

Makes approximately 3 dozen cookies.

index